NEW
WRITING
MATTER
12

GW00602616

MATTER 12

Editors: Tricia Durdey, Kate Rutter

Contributing editors:
Rosemary Badcoe, Neil Baker, Janet Blackwell,
Jamie Coward, Brigidin Crowther, Suzannah Evans,
Kirsty Fisher, Anne Grange, Katie Hook, Andrew
Jeffrey, Mark Kirkby, Margaret Lewis, Andy Martin,
Suzanne McArdle, Ruth Palmer, Pat Phillips, Panni
Pohyokeloh, Mark Thorpe, Denise Setterington,
Anna Smith, Louis Wood

Contents: copyright remains with the
individual authors

Designed by Eleven Design
Web design: Joanna Throup
Image curator: Fay Musselwhite
Photography: Joshua Holt, Karl Hurst,
Mary Musselwhite

Published by Mews Press
Printed by Northend Creative Print Solutions

Special thanks to Glenn Thornley at Eleven Design
Lesley Glaister
Professor Maurice Riordan and Professor Steven
Earnshaw at Sheffield Hallam University

All rights reserved. No part of this publication may
be reproduced or transmitted, in any form or by any
means, electronic or mechanical, including
photocopying, recording or any information storage
or retrieval system without prior permission.

ISBN 978-1-84387-354-9

www.makingwritingmatter.co.uk

MATTER showcases the best work from writers on the MA Writing at Sheffield Hallam University, alongside new poetry and prose from established writers.
This year's guest contributors are poets Ian Duhig and Carola Luther, and novelists Sarah Butler and Michèle Roberts.

Contents

Lesley Glaister
Introduction to Matter 12

Welcome to *Matter 12*, a showcase of the work of students on Sheffield Hallam University's MA in Writing. As a former tutor on this very degree – from its inception in 1993 until 2011– I was particularly delighted to be invited to write an introduction to this collection. And I was even more delighted – and absurdly proud – to see the names of some of my former students amongst the selected writers.

SHU's MA in Writing was among the first tranche of what has become a proliferation of postgraduate writing courses in colleges and universities all over Britain. These vary tremendously in style, content and success and (though I am, of course, a mite biased) I would rate the SHU degree among the very best in terms of the talent and professionalism of its staff, the calibre of its students and the success many of them have gone on to enjoy.

It has become a commonplace criticism of postgraduate writing courses that they operate as a sort of literary equivalent of the sausage machine, taking individually talented writers, indoctrinating them with a particular orthodoxy and churning out strings of uniformly crafted pieces of work. Well, a look through *Matter 12* should quickly disabuse anyone of that idea.

The samples of work here – poetry, short story, novel extract and script – could hardly be more varied in style or subject matter. In these pages we thrill to fresh metaphor, enjoy playful and inventive prosody and beautifully sinuous free verse. We are treated to comedy – surreal, paradoxical and that arising naturally from situation; to various degrees of tragedy and to the precisely realised quotidian. We experience the voice of a nine-year-old girl, a failing comedian, and, most movingly, an Inuit woman as she recounts a traumatic journey through the snow. We see how nature seems to spool back on a journey north and how time fast-forwards us towards old age. We travel (via many clearly evoked corners of Britain) from the Middle East to the frozen north; and time-travel between the 17th and the 21st centuries. We watch a small town bully terrorise his family and see a man fix on and follow young females – for unexpected motives. We die with a trapped pot-holer and experience a rock climb – the words ingeniously employed like precarious toe-holds across the page. And much, much more. So much varied experience, so many different visions, styles and voices – not a single sausage in evidence here!

This collection is complemented – and in no way overshadowed – by the inclusion of lovely works by guest writers Michèle Roberts and Sarah Butler and poets Ian Duhig and Carola Luther. And praise is due to Tricia Durdey and Kate Rutter for the hard work and skill involved in the editing process.

As you read *Matter 12*, prepare to be engrossed, amused, moved, stimulated and above all excited. After all you will be among the first readers privileged to sample the work of some new and very talented writers.

Fay Musselwhite
Eggs

Before we come to term, are drawn
by dryness and light, we lay a store down

the way a merest swell on the pumpkin vine
holds designs to survive its own reach,

and rosebay willow herb pumps clouds.
Our finite supply of ova nestle, primed

to glide inside an opening line
as words awaiting a sentence.

Jenny Vernon
The Stone House

Novel extract from 'The Stone House'

Aliana

I will tell you more if you would like to hear. I can tell
you how my life changed. It was all to do with dogs.
This little puppy and its mother are precious. You don't
understand that. Pakka doesn't really understand that.
Maybe Mukpa knows. He remembers, I think. He must
do, although he doesn't speak of it.

I remember the last trip I made with my husband.
It was spring. My daughter was a toddler, still in my
pouch. Mukpa was a young boy of ten springs – it
would be three years ago. He helped his father hitch the
dogs – our lovely dogs. They were well fed and fat and
ready to go, new boots for their paws, tails up, eyes
bright. A beautiful team. They could find their own way
if you fell asleep on the journey. He helped his father
secure our baggage on the qomatiq. Mukpa was not
strong enough to stretch the rope tight, but Okalik
didn't shame him. He encouraged him, and when the
boy's back was turned he tightened up the bindings
himself. He let little Mukpa keep his pride. 'How else
will he learn if we don't give him confidence?' he said.

My family came out to see us off, and we all said
goodbye there on the shore – you will see what a
beautiful place it is – rich in seals, many walrus on the
islands, fish in the rivers and along the shore, caribou
inland, geese, duck and fox. It is a wonderful place. Not
at all like the Straits. But my husband was needed back
home with his own people. So we set off inland to cross
the passes.

We left it as late as we dared. Neither of us wanted

to go, but no-one can cross if the snow has gone from the trail. We left it until the sea ice began to crack and my family wanted to move camp. We left then.

We had a big load, but the journey was straightforward. We climbed and climbed, over the first pass, down and across the lake. Then we got to the second ascent. Mukpa said he'd seen a bad spirit following us. He'd been sitting on the qomatiq that afternoon, facing backwards, so he could see the country behind us. We left some offerings for the spirits, as we always did when we crossed from one territory to another.

Mukpa became scared. 'It's still after us,' he said. We left more offerings and checked our amulets. They were still safely sewn into our clothing. We said there was nothing to worry about. But we did worry.

Then we saw it too. A single figure with a tiny qomatiq pulled by one dog. He stood out dark against the snow. We stared and stared, but we couldn't make out whether it was an evil torngak, or a helper spirit, or perhaps even a man. Who would travel this way alone? We carried on much longer than we would have liked, on beyond dark. Then we stopped and made a quick night shelter in a snow bank. We all felt rather than saw the figure continuing on towards us. We kept watch, but we were very tired. We settled the dogs outside, tethered away from the qomatiq that carried our supplies, food and furs, and also our tent. We just took in one sleeping robe for the four of us. A caribou robe. Of course I ate it later on. I remember every mouthful.

The last time we had looked before the light failed Okalik said our pursuer looked like that Inuk who came with the white whalers last summer. The angry man. Apak. That was his name. Apak.

We slept, and in the morning Okalik broke out of our shelter to greet the dawn of a new day and feed the dogs. He yelled. I clambered out with my little girl in my arms, and Mukpa came too. I will never forget the horror of what we saw. Our dogs had gone. Our qomatiq had gone, and with it all our food, our tent and dry clothing. Even my lamp and oil supply. We'd been too tired to bring it in and light it the night before. We hadn't thought our pursuer could travel in the gloom.

In its place was the small makeshift qomatiq we'd seen following us. There was no sign of its single dog. And the tracks showed us that Apak, for now we were sure it was him, had continued on up towards the next pass. On towards the Straits, using our equipment and our dogs.

I will stop here. It is too much to tell you. I know you have come across Apak too. I've upset you with my story. But I am tired now. Perhaps Mukpa remembers what happened next. You can ask him if you're interested.

★★★

I said I'd tell you how Mukpa and I got back to my husband's people. After Apak stole our dogs and everything we possessed we could see by his tracks that he'd headed on across the passes towards our Narrow Channel Village. The four of us began to walk in his tracks. But my daughter was heavy and Mukpa slow. My husband could not carry Mukpa far even though he was just a lad. The three of us were holding Okalik back, so we decided that he should travel on alone and fetch help from the coast. He hoped he might meet other travellers coming towards us at that time of year. It was our only hope. Our only chance.

We found a good snow drift and built up a snow shelter to be as weatherproof as possible. As he left he sealed us inside. We lay down and I tried to sleep, like a bear with her cubs, and wait for spring. I cut slivers of the sleeping robe day by day and Mukpa and I chewed on it pretending it was fresh fatty seal meat.

It was not long before my milk dried up. My daughter could not digest the skin, no matter how much I chewed it for her. She died there in my arms as we slept.

I lost track of time passing. Then one afternoon as the light coming in through our snow house began to fail, we heard scratching on the outside of our wall. I thought help must have come, so I shouted 'We're here! Is it you husband? We're in here!'

The scratching stopped. Then it started up again, stronger and faster. I called out once more. But no-one replied – nothing but the sound of frantic scratching and digging broke the silence in that dreadful place. We knew then that it was not human.

During the dark night, whatever it was outside broke through the wall. A small hole at first, then the sound of sniffing. A sniffing spirit coming to eat our souls. We cowered against the furthest wall, but our shelter was so small we could feel chunks of ice showering onto our legs as the – whatever it was – dug and snuffled. We could smell it too. Bad spirit breath huffing in with the cold air that flooded our den.

Then it was in and on top of us. I pushed my son behind me and crouched with my ulu in my hand. It leapt on me and bit my shoulder. I nearly fainted with the pain, but I kept my balance and slashed at the monster. I felt the ulu blade slice through its clothing and into flesh. I slashed again as it drew back. It snarled and came at me again. We fell sideways and wrestled on the floor of that shelter. As we rolled the weight of our bodies broke the wall down where my assailant had scratched the hole.

We tumbled outside and fought on the soft snow. I could hear Mukpa screaming. Of course you did, son, you were just a child. Your screaming saved us from death because hearing you gave me courage to fight. The two of us rolled and wrestled and fought all night. It got in a few more bites, and I got in a few more cuts. It was wearing thick fur clothing, and it was hard to slash through to the flesh beneath. We were well matched in our determination!

But as the sky began to lighten my enemy weakened and, thinking of my son, I found new strength. I climbed astride it out there on the snow, and I cut its throat! I wasn't sure I had killed it. Some of these mountain spirits are impossible to kill. They live in the other world, so they cannot die in ours.

I crawled back into what was left of our shelter, and collapsed. Mukpa, dear boy, tried to build up the broken walls, then he fell asleep against me.

When I awoke I went outside and found a dead wolf bitch in a pool of blood. So you see, we did have food, and a warm, if lacerated, pelt, and somehow we survived for a few more days until Nanuya came looking for Okalik. Instead, he found us, and he could not disguise his disappointment. He never even tried to hide it, but reminded me of it every day until you two, my dear Pakka and Nelson, rescued me and my son.

We never found my husband's body.

Carola Luther
Disturbance

Her breath could be the sea
her mind the sky above the sea
and there to the right a moon.
Full moon in the night-blue sky
full, or near enough
its quietness knitting a scarf
lace, wet, light
and laying it down
for us to walk along
as we cross the sleep-blue sea.

And that? A scratch of black
shaped like a boat, a boat in a print
black ink. Curve, line
figure like a man.
Thin.

Her breath could be the sea
her mind the sky above the sea
and there to the right a moon.

The boat, if it is a boat
has drifted in, the figure of a man
if it is a man, leans down.
He lifts a bundle the size of a lamb
and drops it in.

She waits for the splash.
I wait for the gulping sound of a splash
as water opens
accepts things in.

Breath could be the sea
mind the sky above the sea
and there to the right a moon.
Full moon in the night sky
full, or near enough
its silence knitting a scarf
lace
laying it down
laying it over the blue-black sea.

Carola Luther
Arctic

There were things going on between you like the slow death of something,
a restless mammal shut inside the room, so at first I read a magazine
and faded out to sofa colour, then through the window, watched
a brown moon squat the horizon, and as you collaborated
to make the dinner – *no, no, I couldn't help* – I turned the TV on

sound down, because we already had Michael Nyman playing piano
in the background, and I sat and watched an image of a melt drop
fill the screen, a melt drop weeping at its own release it seemed to me,
and I could've talked to you about the lost contents of that one drop,
of history's disappearing skins, I could have talked of stopped time

unstopped, dispersing here before our eyes, of the singularity,
the sameness of that melt drop's curve, I could have talked of all its sisters
– *watch* – gathering now behind it – *watch* – its moment apprehended,
unexpected – the sudden swell and burst and broken stalk and overspill,
the see-through bleeding, the speeding up of beats of drops, each one hanging

like wet transparent fruit, the way a moonlit, rained-on apple hangs, or a pear
in moonlight. And in my ear some distant source appeared to roar, and *watch*
watch I could have said and didn't say, and now the piano track
had finished, the silence in the kitchen was studded with the clunks and clinks
of table being laid, the thurr thurr of wooden spoon rotating round

the inside of a stainless steel pan, and these became the melt-drop score,
and because I didn't say what I might have said to you, only I was there
to catch that glimpse of blur, that tiny dullness, the little shade of mist
or scum inside, and it could have been pollution, but the breaking taste
of old dead water wasn't that, it was dirt upon my tongue, no not quite

dirt, nor earth or *brak* or rot or salt, not quite metal, not quite plastic,
not pond, or pissed-on ice, not even mammoth dung, powdered coelacanth
or ancient snow, it was more like dust, say of human blood or tears, but grainier,
grainier, the taste that I might imagine would belong to comet spoor,
yes, or the once-whole debris of an imploding star.

Suzanne McArdle
Good Neighbours

The village huddled beneath edgeless skies where earth and sea met. As starlings massed and reeled, she unloaded bean bags and rugs. She slept on the floor, kept T-shirts in bags, until bed and drawers could be landed; prepared to snuggle in, even though the wind blasted three hundred and sixty days of the year.

But the spinster screwed up her face at underwear hung out on Sunday, the bachelor stole glimpses of her pillar-box hair, the retirees shot looks at her slant-parked car. No one offered sugar. Only the spinster's cat took to her.

A man appeared in the corn field. A metallic glint like the sea rose up from the sheaves, not waves, but the spinning hub caps of an upended car. She shouted, but the man's head was tilted, his eyes transfixed by the starlings' soft geometry. She towed him to her joss-scented living room, fingers twitching to dial an ambulance, but there was not a dent on him.

Neighbours circled the skewed metal and watched as the man brought in the milk and dug the front garden. They spat on the pavement and muttered about ungodly hair. In her garden the villagers sniffed out the purple flowers of wolfsbane, or so they claimed. And, though there was television, there were still old ones, who spoke of ancient ways.

For Good Neighbours' Week they set to building a fire, gathering driftwood from the estuary. The giant nest of twigs and logs made her bones crackle. She felt the pull of something old as she dug the soil, not knowing how she could name the yellow flowers of henbane, the shiny black belladonna berries, and the dainty filigree of columbine with poison in its roots.

When her car was gouged with jagged lines she sent the man south. Then she posted housewarming invitations, although the scratched car was packed, the bean bags stowed, the T-shirts and sweaters tucked in.

They came clutching cheap bottles. One of the bonfire builders brought rope, slinging the coiled braid in a corner. The tip reared up like the head of a snake. The cat hissed at it.

Sweet-smelling punch bubbled on the stove. The villagers helped themselves, ladling it into glasses and tea cups. She kept her own separate, miming tiny sips, and then she slipped away. They drank until someone heaved over the aconitum (or wolfsbane, as it was called when the grey ones still crept around the village). She drove south. Birds rose wing-tip to wing-tip. Her neighbours' breath was tight as snagged fishing lines, their lungs flapping like landed fish.

Ruth Palmer
Care
A Short Film

FADE IN:

<u>INT. PUBLIC BUS – LATE AFTERNOON.</u>

> <u>MAN (V.O.)</u>
> I sit on the back seat of the bus. Dress down,
> wear a hood over my skin.

A bedraggled-looking MAN is sitting on the back seat
of a busy bus. It is occupied mainly by schoolchildren.
He wears an oversized scruffy duffle coat, baggy cords
and holey shoes. He looks to the floor and bites on his
lip anxiously. He occasionally looks up at a lone teenage
SCHOOLGIRL, reading a book. He studies her.

> <u>MAN (V.O.)</u>
> I don't do this for fame or praise.

A group of naughty SCHOOLBOYS throw sweet
wrappers at him. He ignores them and sinks further into
his seat. The boys soon stop as they are distracted by
their mobile phones and the man pursues his studying
of the girl.

> <u>MAN (V.O.)</u>
> I love them, ask nothing in return.

The girl puts the book in her rucksack, pulls up her
white school socks and zips up her coat.

The man looks out of the window, looking for the next
stop.

MAN (V.O.)
I pick my girl with care. She must be young.
Alone. Show no signs of being touched.

The girl presses the button for the next stop and stands,
places some headphones into her ears and presses play
on her MP3 player.

The man waits a few seconds and then pulls his hood
up and walks to the front of the bus.

The naughty boys notice and point at his holey shoes.

SCHOOLBOY 1
Can't you afford new shoes?
Fucking tramp!

SCHOOLBOY 2
You stink old man! Get a bath.

The group laugh. The man ignores them. He stares at
the back of the girl's head as she nods to the rhythm of
her music.

The bus stops.

MAN (V.O.)
When she gets off the bus I tag along.

The girl steps off the bus, so does the man.

EXT. SUBURBAN STREET – AFTERNOON.

It is starting to get dark.

The BUS DRIVER waits for the girl to cross the road
in front of the bus, waving her across the street, smiling.

She rushes across the road.

The man stands at the bus-stop and watches the bus drive away and then begins to follow the girl.

MAN (V.O.)
It's a question of keeping the right distance.

The man maintains the same distance between himself and the girl until she reaches the entrance to a public park.

EXT. DESERTED PARK – AFTERNOON.

The man stands unseen in the shadows of the park's gates as the girl enters the park.

She stops for a few seconds to change the track on her MP3 player.

A drunken TRAMP stumbles over to her.

TRAMP
Any change for a cuppa love?

The girl is startled and pulls the earphones quickly from her ears.

GIRL
Um...No. Sorry.

She rushes onwards as the tramp mumbles and hobbles back to a park bench. She looks back to where the tramp approached her and the man quickly edges himself into the hedgerow, remaining unseen. She places the headphones back in and continues to walk.

The man exhales deeply and continues to follow her, lessening the gap between them. Soon he is within half a metre of her. He strokes the air behind her head as if stroking her hair.

EXT. SUBURBAN STREET – AFTERNOON.

The street is busy with pedestrians, cars and bikes. The girl looks both ways before starting to cross the busy road. As she steps out, a fast car appears to come from nowhere so she quickly steps back.

The man gasps on seeing the near miss.

She crosses the street to her home on the other side and disappears through the front door.

MAN (V.O.)
I see her safe to her home.

The man watches from a bus-stop on the opposite side of the street as the GIRL'S MOTHER hugs her in a lit-up living room window.

A WOMAN in the bus-stop queue sticks her arm out to stop an approaching bus.

INT. PUBLIC BUS – EARLY EVENING.

The man sits on the back seat of the bus.

MAN (V.O.)
Then catch another bus, begin again.

He looks to the floor and bites on his lip anxiously. He occasionally looks up at a lone FEMALE UNIVERSITY STUDENT, eating a sandwich. He studies her between looking back to the floor.

EXT. A GRASS FIELD – NIGHTTIME

A YOUNGER LOOKING MAN is lying on his back,

his legs and arms spread outwards and his eyes closed.
He is dressed smartly. A briefcase beside him is open,
its paper contents are being blown about by the breeze.
A collection of empty alcohol bottles surrounds him.
The grass is frosty.

<u>MAN (V.O.)</u>
My path was revealed to me in a dream.
Naked, I followed a girl across the city. A
chrysalis of frost formed on my skin. Stars
blinked morse as I left my body.

He is holding a newspaper. Its front page is blown
upwards towards a starry sky and a cityscape. We see a
photo of the man pictured with a teenage girl, both
smiling. The headline reads:

'Father Makes Emotional Appeal For Missing
Daughter.'

The front page blows swiftly away towards the city.

THE END

Kate Rutter
Heading North

Bank holiday Monday at Buckshaw Parkway
and one woman alights in a well-worn anorak.
Those who stay are the time travellers
on a trip to where the daffs still stand erect
like rows of big band trumpeters. At Preston
the shock of broom vanishes from embankments,
trees suck back their leaves in an intake of breath
and blossom closes its perfume into a fist.
We cross the border and slip another week.
Flat-capped dunrocks start to unwind their nests
and give back the moss they stole from gutterings.
The sky descends like a Glasgow dustbin lid.
We breach the barrier and file into the dark
as hills fill up their pockets with last-minute snow.

Suzannah Evans
The Chernobyl Circus

At Pripyat the elephants cried
and got diarrhoea.
The troupe hefted their luggage,
looked up at a storm sky.

In town men in green suits
hosed the asphalt. Shy of news,
the radio played symphonies
for three full days.

The clowns were funnier
than they'd ever been.
The contortionist's body
bent like metal in a fire.

The trapeze artists clung
to each other's hands
and flew like swallows
in a forest of burned trees.

Sarah Butler
Bride or Groom?

Once the grass between the gravestones has been
trampled with confetti colours, and the photographer
has worked his way through his script, we are herded
onto a coach with balloons tied to the windscreen
wipers. The best man, who has rugby player shoulders
beneath his navy suit, stands at the coach door.

'Whoa, whoa.' He holds up a hand as I approach.
'The important thing at this point is your badge. Do you
have it?'

The pale pink rosette had been tucked, without
explanation, inside the expensive-looking order-of-
service given to me at the church door. I fumble in my
handbag and hold it up for inspection.

'Good, good. Hop on.'

I take a window seat half way down the coach.
Outside, Rachel and Mark stand, smiles fixed to their
faces, his hand on the small of her back. Another
wedding party is already congregating at the church
door. Rachel wears white. Two pale blue ribbons hold
the dress together in a criss-crossed line all the way up
her spine. Tiny blue embroidered flowers reach around
the neckline, and her hair is scooped up, God alone
knows how, so just two dark curls skim the edges of her
face.

A man in his forties, with a discernible paunch,
takes the seat next to me.

'Beautiful day for it,' he says.

I nod.

'What do you think about this name idea, then?'

He pulls a handkerchief from his pocket and wipes
his face. I watch him rub the creased cotton across his
eyes and forehead, and remember the woman in the pew

in front of me, who cried during the vows, and immediately drew a finger underneath each eye, inspecting it for traces of mascara. I've never been much of a one for make-up. John used to buy me sets of it for my birthday. I did try, those first few years, but I've never understood how women use those things up; a year would turn and you'd think I'd hardly touched it. He kept at it, stocking my dressing table with plastic-encased rainbows. I'm not a colouring book, I shouted, once. I just want you to care, he said. We had different ideas about things.

'I mean, tradition's tradition isn't it?' the man says. 'I know these young ones like mucking things around, but sometimes I think they're just doing it for the sake of it.'

The coach slides away from the kerb.

'How do you mean?' I ask.

'Well, it gets confusing, doesn't it? Women keep their names, and then what happens with the kids? We're breeding a race of people with so many surnames they have to keep them together with hyphens. I suppose that's why these two have decided it's one way or the other. But still –'

I remember the first time I signed a cheque with my new name. The ink on the page told me I was a different person, but I felt exactly the same. By the time I had a piece of paper confirming the divorce, it was too late; my old name was so faint, so far away, so overwritten with his name, I didn't feel able to take it back.

The rugby player makes his way to the front of the coach, finds a microphone from somewhere and turns to face us.

'Ladies and Gentlemen.' A cheer swirls around the coach. I am sitting in direct sunlight and can feel the beginnings of a headache scratch at my temples. 'Boys and girls. Do you all have your badges?' A murmur of assent; pink and blue rosettes are held aloft. 'Please attach them to your lapel, your bosom, your hat, your handbag, and listen carefully.'

The man next to me fumbles with the tiny safety pin on his blue rosette. I leave mine in my bag.

'You are invited, friends of Rachel and Mark, to help decide whose surname they will take into their married life.' Cheers, whoops, laughter. 'We stand, ladies and gentleman, at a cross-roads, on a bridge if you like. We are of a time when a man might take a woman's name as easily as she might take his.'

The man next to me turns and raises his eyebrows. I frown and clap as loudly as I can. I let a quiet 'woo-hoo' escape my lips, hardly loud enough for anyone to hear.

'The badges show your teams,' the man at the front of the coach continues. 'Ladies are pink, gentlemen are blue. If the pinks win, Mark takes Rachel's name. If the blues win, Rachel takes Mark's name. Simple.'

The coach pulls into the long driveway of the hotel. It takes several seconds before the building comes into view – a turreted red brick façade, tall windows looking onto a cropped, well-watered lawn. Imagine it: a man taking his wife's name. Simple, he said, a matter so insubstantial it can be decided by team games on a summer's afternoon.

There is champagne in fluted glasses, and slightly tasteless canapés. It's like a school sports day, with a wooden table at the edge of the lawn, and an officious-looking woman telling people what to do. I stand on my own, and sip my drink as slowly as I can. I wonder why I came in the first place; being on your own at a wedding is never fun, despite what they say, and all this nonsense with egg-and-spoon races and staggering around with a book on your head doesn't suit me at all. Even so, as the afternoon drifts on, I can't help but notice how the atmosphere changes; the laughter shifts into cries of victory or disappointment; there are definite hushes before scores are announced. I am an old woman; I've never been one for games, but this is different, I realise. I finish my drink, attach the fiddly pink rosette to the maroon silk of my blouse, and make my way to the table. I am told to stand still. A man ties my ankle to another woman's ankle with a pink strip of material.

'Mrs Morley,' he says. 'I remember you.'

Kevin Maher. He was bright, did Physics at University, I think. I want to say, it's Ms Staunton, actually. Instead, I say, 'Kevin, how are you?'

'Not bad, not bad. Stand still now, we'll have no cheating. Serious stuff, this.'

My team mate wears silver heels which sink into the hotel lawn. We're next to the man from the coach. His face shines with sweat. His leg is tied to a young man with the same dark hair and pronounced cheekbones as Rachel. They get ahead straight away. We curse and stumble along. 'Bastard,' my team mate mutters, 'bastard, bastard shoes.'

Rachel and Mark flit between the groups clustered on the lawn. I talk to a boy I used to teach; he's telling me about his kids, but I can't concentrate. The tension is almost palpable. The heat, perhaps, or the champagne, or just a rising desire, by those who wear a pink ribbon fashioned into a flower, to change something.

A huddle of people stand around the desk. The games have stopped. The officious woman has a smirk painted across her face. On the table in front of her, a length of rope lies coiled like a snake. The rugby player picks up a handheld bell, and rings it.

'Ladies and Gentlemen; pinks and blues.' The crowd hushes quickly. 'We have come to the end of our games.' I grab another glass of champagne from a passing teenager in a white shirt. I am finding it difficult to breathe. 'And it falls to me to announce –' He pauses, playing his audience. 'That the scores currently stand – at a draw.' Murmurs, the crowd shifts. 'There is nothing for it, ladies and gentlemen.' He lifts the rope above his head. 'We must have a decider. I invite each and every one of you to flex your muscles, gird your loins, and join the tug of war.'

Yells and whoops and laughter. But it isn't funny, I realise, as I watch the pinks separate from the blues. We are a colourful team, a pack of butterflies in our dresses, with our bare arms, rainbow necklaces, and high-heeled shoes; we are seriously disadvantaged.

I glance across at Rachel and Mark, who are standing, his arm around her shoulders, her eyes fixed on her girls. She's smiling, but surely she can see it's a set up. I take my place, behind a girl who can't be more than seven years old. A tall woman wearing a dark purple dress heads up the team. She turns and surveys us.

'We're going to do this,' she says, and there is steel in her voice. 'Dig your heels in, pull hard, and when I shout Rachel, let up just a fraction until they think they've got us, and then pull. For Rachel.'

'For Rachel,' we chant, and there's a sudden flash of energy amongst us. I wipe my hands on my skirt and curl them around the rope.

The officious-looking woman, who doesn't wear a badge of either colour, holds up her hand: 'On my count of three. One. Two. Three.'

And we pull. I try to weight myself down through the soles of my feet. I curse my practical shoes, long for the sharp heels of my team mates which punch into the soil like anchors. The blue team grunts and heaves, like they're rowing a ship. From our team though, the noise is a constant, rising tone, a desperate, determined yell that I realise is coming from my throat too; my mouth open and the roar of it resonating through my body. The rope rips at my hands. The sweat seeps into my bra, drips like a line of tears down the length of my back.

'Rachel.'

We do as we've been told, and a cry of victory starts to swell from the opposite side.

'Now!'

I feel the surge of power. Heels dug into earth, muscles straining at their edges. I can see sweat slicked across the shoulders of the women in front.

'They're moving,' someone shouts, and it's true. We start to shift backwards in a tumbling, stumbling, victorious line.

'Rache – el.'

We take her name and stretch it into a victory chant. I stand, shaking with adrenaline, and watch the woman in the purple dress and three others sprint towards Rachel and Mark. They lift her onto their shoulders and run, in a flurry of coloured silk, on a lap of the grounds. Rachel grins and punches the air, glancing over her shoulder at her new husband. I follow her gaze. The look on his face tells me what I really should have expected, and when she returns and he leans close to whisper something to her, the snap of tension across her shoulders confirms it. My headache returns, champagne-tight around my skull. My arms ache with wasted effort.

I don't want to know. By the time I hear from her again – my yearly Christmas card update – a hundred other compromises will have been made. I want to leave thinking it's true: that a man could take his wife's name, as easily as she might take his. I want to leave thinking it's that simple.

The dinner's a buffet affair. There are no name cards to declare my betrayal. I unpin my pink rosette, take my bag from the silver coat rack, and slip away.

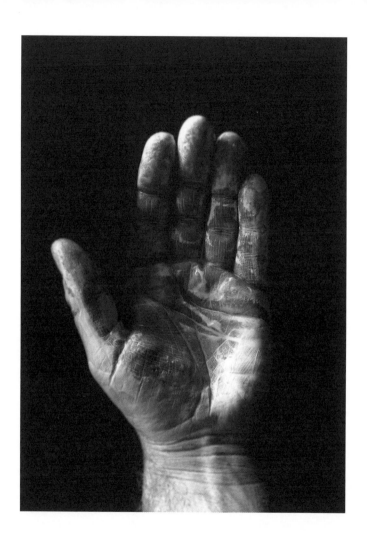

Ian Duhig
The Balladeer's Lament

My forms will never warm these hares;
  not here nor there, they turn again
their free verse from my poem's course
  for mazes their own brains lay down.

They slip my words as easily
  as they their shapes and English gods
to please themselves, the world a breeze;
  still new their tricks, too old this dog.

(a form is a hare's nest).

Ian Duhig
Long Will

Langland's my name   long gone from this land
where lettered and lout   alike my tongue lashed;
I'd flay fellow-clerics   for failing their flocks
as fast as the riff-raff   for riot and wrath,
as fiercely as princes   who prey on the poor –
wealth is mere theft   wed into or won,
inherited wealth   as heinous a haul,
inherited wits too   a wonder as worthless
when wasted in words   not wisdom, good works.
My poem gave watchwords   to Wat's men and women
who rose in rebellion   against England's wrongs.
Now I'm brought back   by a fart of a bard,
to rage and to rant   in my *rum, ram, ruff* staves –
a rough and rude roar   in my own raw era,
a savage sound now   upon this sod's soft ears.
I'll make his ears smart   our sorryarse sinner,
a smug poetaster,   posturing pen-pusher
who'd write off religion   as simply a relic
of spent superstitions   from centuries past.
He'd sneer at the prayers   of penitent paupers
whose hope in His heaven   is all hope they have;
he'll tell you that medicine   mends all ill men.
What pills or potions   preserve poisoned souls?
What exercise exorcises   enmity's sins?
Paul's letters that kill   are the kind of this clerk,
vanity's vessel,   void of all spirit.
Where I look with longing   for lines true and straight,
the pen cutting plain   as Piers Ploughman's share,
unveeringly drawn   from verse-end to verse-end,
I find instead fiddling   as fancy as Frenchmen's
or rhyme chancer Chaucer   chose for his poesy;
where I seek rhythms   rum, rough and ramming,

wholesome and heavy   as plough-horse's hooves,
I'm bored stiff by beatless,   babyish rattlings,
unmeasured metre   men's feet can't march to;
no clashing of consonants   but cowardly vowels
softening such combat   to simpering songs.
His maundering minstrelsy's   destined for mulch,
pulp spread like gullshit   in Piers Ploughman's wake,
feeding His fields   for heavenly bread
whose hymns and hosannas   will rise sweet and high
when people will praise   without poets' help
the grandeur and glory   of God and His works.
For this I'd give thanks.   Give thought to my themes.

*'Long Will' was a nickname for William Langland, whose
'Piers Ploughman' was indeed quoted by Wat Tyler and his
fellow rebels. It seems to have maintained a particular
attraction for Northern writers down to Ted Hughes and,
more recently, Simon Armitage. This poem imitates, honours
and takes a few liberties with that tradition.*

Mark Kirkby
Show Home

A Short Film

EXT. SUBURBAN STREET – NIGHT

A car, a black Golf Mk4, crawls down a suburban
street. Tyres squeeze against the kerb.

INT. CAR – NIGHT

Inside the Mk4 are SPIKE and TRACE, a couple in
their late teens. Spike drives. Trace, visibly pregnant, is
studying colour charts and home furnishing magazines,
when -

                    TRACE
        Wait...

The car slows to a halt. Nothing they do is too quick.

                    TRACE
        Back up.

Spike slots the car into reverse. Trace moves her jaw in
time with the clunk of the gears.

The car crawls backwards, coming to a halt outside a
suburban house with its curtains open. The living room
light spills over the pavement and into their car.

Trace looks down at her dress. The light is edging onto
it, curving over her bump. She traces the line of it with
her finger.

                                TRACE
         Feel that.

Spike reaches over and puts his hand in the light,
turning it round as if warming it.

                                SPIKE
         Mmmm.

EXT. PAVEMENT – NIGHT

Trace and Spike get out of the car, stand on the
pavement and look inside the house. They close their
eyes and bathe in the light, as if it's a sun lamp.

                                TRACE
         Shall we?
                                SPIKE
         I think so.

They brush each other's hand. Trace takes a hanky
from her pocket.

EXT. SIDE DOOR TO HOUSE – NIGHT

Spike knocks on the door. The door is opened by a
man, PAUL, in his thirties.

                                PAUL
         Hello?

Trace dabs the hankie to her face.

                                PAUL
         Are you OK?

                                SPIKE
         Travel sickness. We couldn't...my girlfriend.
         Clean up?

Paul looks Spike up and down, then catches sight of Trace's bump.

> PAUL
>
> Oh...yeah, sure. This way.

Spike waits outside as Paul leads Trace to the toilet. As soon as they are out of sight, Spike steps inside.

INT. KITCHEN – NIGHT

With eyes fixed on the light spilling from the living room, Spike tears off his trainers to reveal bare feet. He lets the trainers fall to the kitchen floor as he heads for the living room.

INT. LIVING ROOM – NIGHT

Paul's wife, AMY, is watching TV as Spike walks straight into the living room.

> AMY
>
> Hello?

Spike ignores her. He closes his eyes and runs his fingers over the wallpaper. He puts his hand on the bulbs in the ceiling lamp. There is a little sizzle of skin burning, but Spike doesn't flinch. His bare feet clench the carpet. He breathes in the scent of the AirWick.

> AMY
>
> What the fuck are you...? PAUL?

> SPIKE
>
> We like your room here. We like it very much.

Amy tries to drag Spike out of the room. Spike, surprisingly strongly for a skinny kid, easily holds her at arm's length.

Paul walks into the room and tries to drag Spike off Amy.

Spike strains to get over to the floor-standing lamp in the corner of the room, but Paul holds him back. Spike gets his fingertips to the lamp, but can only knock it over.

PAUL

> Get out. Get OUT.

Spike violently cranes his neck to try get a view of the floor standing lamp as Paul forces him out of the room.

EXT. DRIVEWAY TO HOUSE – NIGHT

Paul throws Spike out into the drive, where Trace is waiting under the street light.

Spike moves round to the front of the house to look in through the window. He presses his fingers to the glass until the skin goes white.

INT. LIVING ROOM – NIGHT

Amy, terrified, turns her back on Spike.

Paul enters the room, closes the curtains and moves away from Amy. They don't look at each other.

AMY

> What just happened?

Paul tries to pick up the lamp, but it's suddenly heavy and he can't.

AMY

> Speak to me.

INT. KITCHEN – NIGHT

Paul and Amy don't notice Spike's trainers sprawled out on their kitchen floor.

INT. CAR – NIGHT

Spike and Trace are back in the Mk4. Spike is driving slowly. Their faces show no sign of what has just happened.

> TRACE
> Nice people.

> SPIKE
> Lovely. Really lovely.

> TRACE
> Walls?

> SPIKE
> Anaglypta with a forest floor finish.

Trace pulls out the relevant colour chart and circles a colour.

> TRACE
> Main light?

Spike runs his thumb over his palm.

> SPIKE
> Sixty watt powersave.

Trace writes the details down in a notepad.

> TRACE
> Floor lamp?

Spike shakes his head, 'no'.

                    TRACE
         Well, next time.

                    SPIKE
         I left my trainers.

They look at each other. Trace smiles and contentedly
rubs her bump. Spike's bare feet operate the car pedals.

The Mk4 suddenly does a U-turn in the road. The tyres
screech violently. An extensive collection of DIY and
home furnishing catalogues slide across the back seat.

EXT. SUBURBAN STREET – NIGHT

The car pulls up outside Paul and Amy's house, but the
house is now in darkness. Trace shivers. Spike puts a
blanket around her, then gets out of the car and walks
up the drive. The house door is open. He walks in.

INT. KITCHEN – NIGHT

Spike picks up his trainers. The house is silent.

INT. LIVING ROOM – NIGHT

Spike walks into the living room. There is a stain on the
wallpaper, like damp has begun to bloom on it. In the
corner of the room, Paul is desolately holding a glass of
wine.

                    PAUL
         What the fuck did you do? Who are you
         people?

Spike goes over to the floor standing lamp. It is still on
its side.

                              PAUL
        Just take it.

Spike considers, then –
                              SPIKE
        No. I don't think so.

Spike leaves the room.

INT. CAR – NIGHT

Spike gets into the Mk4.

                              TRACE
        Did you get it?

                              SPIKE
        I don't want you to go in there.

                              TRACE
        Something we did?

                              SPIKE
        What did we do? We only took some ideas.

Spike reaches over and holds Trace's hand tenderly.

                              SPIKE
        He called us people.

                              TRACE
        I like that.

Spike slowly releases the hand brake.

                              SPIKE
        Where next?

TRACE

There.

Trace points through the windscreen towards a distant cluster of street lights and houses.

EXT. SUBURBAN STREET – NIGHT

The Mk4 heads off towards the lights, still slowly, always slowly, never rushing.

THE END

Matt Clegg
From **Chinese Lanterns**

Aphorisms make me bite my tongue.
I'm bored with Confucius and Lao Tzu.
I'm tired of white rice and jasmine tea.
    I'll get blind drunk
and walk out into the dusk-city.
I want streets narrow between terraces
and paths pink with blossom smears.
    No more sober thoughts.
I want to be a Chinese lantern.
I want to float through liquorice clouds
steaming above the Bassett's factory.
I want to be a man with tattoos
green and dense as new-sprung leaves.
    A shivering aspen
under moons round as open wells.

Rosemary Badcoe

The Concert

Hendrick ter Brugghen (1626)

Intense as a conspiracy, coiled
and drawn into the corner:
three musicians, a single candle.

The boy sings the beating of their blood,
hand focussed on the fall of notes,
eyes sightless past the taper's glow.

The flautist feels the fall of dark upon his neck;
swings with fingers raised to scrutinise the room
across the starry glint of grapes.

Hair bound in white, the third turns light
upon her cheek and twists, lips parted.
Air moves uneasily, a rearrangement

stirred at the rise of song, disturbed
by the crack of secret papers
bound into the softness of their sleeves,

a vial of poison slipped
beneath the cover of the lute,
dripped into red Venetian wine.

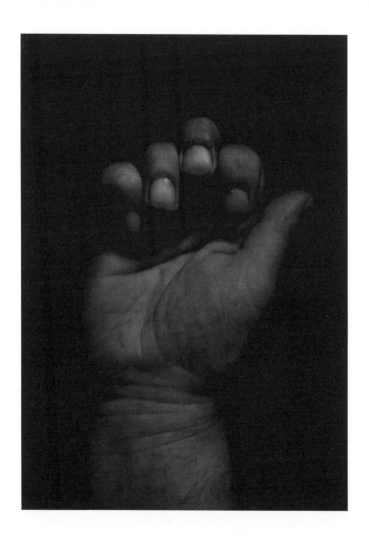

David Buckley
Logan

Novel extract from *'Stone and Water'*

Tommy Logan strode down Fore Street leaving Exeter Cathedral glowing in the sun behind him. Thick-set and above average height he looked like a workman. He had a large round head, bald on top with the remaining hair clipped short at the sides, and he kept himself clean-shaven. Knowing how he looked was part of the job. His people were scared of him. Wary. He knew why, and he intended to keep it that way, but they were silly. They had nothing to fear if they behaved properly. He was a moral man and he didn't want to hurt anyone, even though sometimes it was necessary. The sun reflected off the PVC of his donkey jacket's shoulders as he walked. He had respect for people who worked. Who fixed things. It was just that he didn't need to anymore.

'Paper, Mr Logan?'

The newspaper seller was standing by the art dealer's. His stone-coloured mackintosh was fraying at the bottom.

'Thanks, Alfie.'

Logan took the *Express & Echo* and held out a few coins.

'That's all right Mr Logan. It's on the house.'

'I owe you, Alfie,' said Logan walking on, though Alfie owed Logan for seeing off some teds who'd tormented him on his evening pitch.

Halfway down the steep street leading to the river, a boy of about eighteen appeared from an alleyway. His hair was moulded into a fashionable quiff and he wore a pale blue jacket a size too big for him.

'Do you think you'll grow into that, Stanley?' said Logan, affably.

'It's the fashion, Mr Logan.'

Logan put his arm round the boy's shoulders in a crushing half-embrace.

'Good lad,' he said. 'Now what have you got for me?' The last race had finished an hour before, and Stanley had settled the bets he'd taken for Logan that day.

'Forty-seven pounds, six and eightpence, Mr Logan. I've paid out the winners.'

Logan released his embrace and the boy dug into his jacket pocket. He pulled out a dog-eared black notebook with a rubber band round it. Bank notes stuck out at one end. Stanley dug in again and pulled out a handful of coins.

'Here's the six and eightpence.'

Stanley dropped the coins into his boss's hand. It was twice the size of the boy's.

Logan pocketed the change and took the notebook. He pinged off the rubber band.

'It's all there, Mr Logan,' said the boy hastily.

Logan opened the book and took out the money.

'When someone says it's all there, it makes me think they mean it isn't.'

'It's all there, Mr Logan. I wouldn't, honest.'

Logan paused, looked at the notebook with its pencilled list of horses, odds and amounts wagered, and ran his finger down the last page, the bets for next day.

'I balanced the book, for you, Mr Logan. Apart from the favourite, Mortimer's Run. I laid it at three to one like you said. Everyone wants it. You'll be in trouble if that wins the big one tomorrow.'

'It won't.'

Logan put the notebook in the inside pocket of his donkey jacket. 'So what have you got to tell me?' Logan put his hand on Stanley's shoulder, then lifted it to pat his cheek, a little too heavily to be friendly. 'You're a nice-looking boy,' he said. 'Remember who looks after you.'

'I saw your daughter coming out of the flicks this

afternoon, Mr Logan. The Odeon.'

Logan froze.

'And which of my daughters would that be?'

'The youngest one. Jennifer. She's the tall one, isn't she? Yeah, Jennifer.'

He'd known it would be Jenny. Wendy wouldn't dare.

'Alone or with a boy?'

'On her own, Mr Logan. Running down the road.'

Maybe, thought Logan. But Stanley would be afraid of delivering bad news. Logan had a nose for people's worst motives. He nodded.

'Good lad, Stanley.'

Stanley looked relieved.

'No takers for Sunset Cruiser ante-post, Mr Logan. You only had him at twenties'

'Her. She's a mare.'

'They were offering a hundred to one on the course. She can't win at that price.'

'The price doesn't stop them winning.'

So Stanley had been taking his own bets on the horse, running a sidebook offering bigger odds. He'd let it go, for now. The boy hadn't known what he meant when he said the price didn't stop them winning. But Stanley would find out when Sunset Cruiser won, as Logan had made sure it would. He was completing the boy's education. And he was proud that he didn't have to use violence to do it.

***

When he burst through the door of the isolated terrace house marooned by wartime bombing, Wendy, Jenny and his wife Mary were standing in line, their backs against the sideboard. Beyond lay the little offshot kitchen where they had prepared his tea. He always ate separately, and they would eat afterwards, as he'd decreed. He took in their faces. There was always that look when they had something they didn't want him to find out. But he had found out. He'd make them wait. Logan sat down at the dining table where his place was already laid.

Wendy stepped forward first, pouring a bottle of beer as she'd been told, letting the beer trickle down the inside of the glass so the head would not be too frothy. Jenny went into the cramped kitchen and returned with a casserole dish she placed before him. Logan's wife spoke.

'Jenny used the rabbit you caught yesterday.'

Logan lifted the lid and let the aroma rise. Jenny was trying to buy his approval in case he heard about her illicit cinema trip.

'Very much appreciated. Wendy's turn to cook, wasn't it?'

Mary and the girls looked at each other.

'Jenny really wanted to cook it for you,' said his wife.

'As a special treat for you, Dad,' said Jenny.

Logan grunted. He'd let it ride for now.

When he'd finished he pushed his plate away. It was a signal for his pudding. Jenny produced a jam roly-poly as quickly as a magician's rabbit, put the dish on the table and began cutting the crusty end Logan loved. Her movements were anxious and quick, eager to please. She eased a spatula underneath the pastry roll, cracking through where the jam had just begun to burn onto the dish, and placed it on a bowl.

'Custard?' said Logan. The familiar white jug was not on the table.

The three women looked at each other in panic. Logan looked at them sadly.

'I can't eat it without custard,' he said. 'See what happens when you don't stick to the rota. In the yard.'

Jenny and Wendy looked at each other.

'Both of you,' said Logan.

They turned into the kitchen and towards the back door. Wendy looked back at him appealingly.

'I was going to cook, Dad. Jenny stopped me.'

Logan was disappointed in them. No loyalty, even to each other.

'The yard,' he said, 'both of you.'

Jenny opened the glass-panelled door which led out from the kitchen. Logan followed his daughters out into the bare yard. A chain looped out of a shed at the far end and was cemented into the high red brick walls which enclosed the concreted space. Logan himself had added the top courses of bricks to raise the wall from its original six foot height. He liked privacy.

The chain rattled when something moved in the shed, but Logan's shout silenced it.

Jenny stood facing Logan. He couldn't read her expression. He could read Wendy's. She was usually afraid. Wendy loved him and didn't like his disapproval. Jenny was the one he had to educate more.

'Wendy, up to your room.' Wendy looked relieved and slipped past him back to the kitchen door. 'I'll be up soon,' he said over his shoulder, keeping his gaze fixed on Jenny. 'You know I need to train you,' he said.

He didn't like the way Jenny stared back at him. He'd seen that look before, in the face of the missing daughter he forbade them to talk about or name.

'Haven't you something else to tell me?'

'I don't think so,' she said calmly.

'About films?'

She stayed silent. She was stubborn. She said nothing where other people would lie. She'd been like that since she was little. Now at seventeen she was the same. Other fathers would have beaten it out of her. But he wouldn't. Not personally. Not directly. He had other methods. He felt the anger rising. The power of anger. But he wouldn't let it out. He just had to let people know it was there.

'Keeper,' he called.

The chain rattled again. The shed shook and a large mastiff weighing seven stone emerged. There was a spark of fear in Jenny's eye, but she wouldn't let him know any more than that.

Logan went to the dog, undid the chain from the collar and pointed towards Jenny. The dog began to growl. Jenny backed up against the wall.

'Three hours,' he said.

She knew he meant it. He always meant it. Jenny would stay where she was, knowing Keeper would not touch her if she stayed still. For now she just stared at him. He knew that look. It was the look Dawn used to give him before she ran away. But he knew he could always break them. Even Dawn. In the end, she'd be his again.

Logan didn't knock when he went into Wendy's room. She was sitting on her bed, waiting for him, as he knew she would be. He was always reliable. He was known for his reliability.

'Wendy,' he said. 'You know I'm hurt.'

'Yes, Daddy. I'm sorry.'

'I have to train you.'

'Yes, Daddy.'

'Why didn't you make Jenny stick to the rota.'

Wendy looked down at her slippered feet.

'You're the oldest. You should have controlled her. There's an authority in a house. Look at me.'

She raised her head.

'You'll stay in this room until tomorrow morning. You've got your chamber pot.'

'Yes, Daddy.'

'I'll see you tomorrow. You'll be safe. I need to know you're safe.'

Downstairs in the dark backroom Logan's wife was sitting at the dining table with a plate in front of her. She stopped chewing and looked up nervously, frozen, her knife and fork angled towards each other, her hands at either side of her plate.

'Did I say you could have that?' said Logan, leaning over her, both hands on the table. With a quick scoop of his right hand he flipped her plate over like a tiddlywink, sending it off the end of the table leaving a mess of meat, gravy and pastry on the pretty tablecloth.

'Eat it cold with the girls in the morning if you can't keep the house in order.'

Logan's wife still held her knife and fork either side of the empty space in front of her. He quickly stepped behind her and slapped her on the back. The chunk of meat in her mouth flew out and onto the table.

'Get that lot cleaned up,' he said. 'You're not eating anything till morning.'

Logan's wife screamed at the table, at the wall opposite, at the fate of her children.

'You'll drive them away, like Dawn!'

Logan turned and hit her round the head from the back, so hard she fell to the floor with her chair.

Sometimes violence was necessary.

Margaret Lewis
Becoming a Hill

Stretched thin and pinned
by rock between my shoulder blades
I lie in darkness in a river under Castleton
my wetsuit ripped and gloves in shreds,
one cheek pressed against the smooth rock stream bed
the other grazed by gritstone from above.

I cannot move my head
and water gurgles in one ear,
drowning thoughts of grass and sunshine.

My mouth's submerged.
One nostril flares above the surface:
I slow my breathing,
calm my heartbeat.

I smell dead underground.

I have no toes, numb
fingers spread
ahead in search of space or light.

My veins are river.
My cold bones turn to stone.

Linda Fulton
Seven Easter Eggs

A flash of white robes at the top of the stairs. I knew right away it was Him. Jesus Christ. Didn't Our Lord know everything? And anything He might miss – Himself being busy with his flock and so many sinners and all – then surely His Holy Mother would inform Him.

Looking back, I realise no one would have bothered if I'd told them, the family well used to a child's imaginings. Had I not discovered the little people in the cabbage patch, faeries asleep in furled blankets of green? And once seen the silhouettes of reindeer 'cross a Christmas Eve moon? Such was the magic then in the flicker of a young girl's eye. But on that fine April Monday, I kept Jesus to myself.

I'd only run inside to grab my coat from the peg in the hall, not to linger, not to look. We needed no pilgrims here, no wailing girls, no crawling on hands and knees to any sacred spot of my making. Was there not enough upheaval at home already, and the sitting room packed with a council of relatives? Their whispering and mumbling and Mammy's soft weeping. Though my cheeks burned and my lips quivered, I was no cry baby. In any case, it was only the one glimpse I'd had. Perhaps just a swish of Holy Hem. Nothing Uncle Pat or Father Keenan need be worrying about.

'On these occasions,' I heard Uncle say, 'is it not a fella's duty to chip in a few shillings? So I've sent for Ma Devlin already. The woman does a lovely job of the laying-out.'

Was there to be a party? And what would Jesus think about that, I wondered.

I slammed the door and was away, my heart drumming a faster beat, much quicker than the regular thud I noticed when my head lay on the pillow. I put on the roller skates I'd left on the garden path and with a rumbling of worn wheels and my head spinning, I raced along the pavement slabs, pumping my arms to be all the faster. Ma Devlin in her headscarf passed me on the old black bike with the handlebar basket; the basket, I'd once heard it said, carried her shopping and *mysterious ways*.

It was only a minute before I was back at Aunt Bridie's at the end of the street, where Uncle Pat had said I should stay for a while – at least until Mammy was feeling better and things were seen to. He'd said I was nine years old now, old enough to put Mammy's feelings before my own. To be strong. 'There's a good girl, Mary.'

Later that night, in Aunt's cold spare bed, trying not to listen to my heart in my ears and kept awake by the solemn tick-tocking of the case clock below, I thought maybe I should at least have looked The Lord in the eye. I imagined His arms outstretched, a half-smile on His lips; His long hair curling on His Holy Shoulders. Forgiving. 'I am the Light of the World,' he might say – and I'd wonder, where were His blue cloak and lantern, and I'd ask if He'd come to bring a miracle.

The thing was, I'd eaten six of my seven Easter eggs, and wasn't gluttony a deadly sin? Father Keenan had said so. I had laid the eggs out in a row in my bedroom, moving the books from the shelf to the floor to make a space, displaying my chocolate collection in order, from the first I would eat to the last. From the smallest to the largest – and that egg so magnificent I would leave it for as long as I could resist the temptation. So I'd made a list, giving them names like *the one in the china chicken egg-cup* and *the fat one in the purple foil*. And I'd decided I'd eat them all by myself and tick them off as I did so.

The seventh egg was a marvel: a shell of milk chocolate so delicately iced with plump buds of Lily of the Valley. And the turquoise box lined with yellow satin, and the lid bound with a matching silken bow and fashioned with a hinge so I could open it and close it easily. Open and close. Open and close. I stared at that miracle of chocolate over and over. And through the crinkled orange cellophane I could touch and trace the letters with my finger: frosty joined-up letters, tinged with a golden hue from the wrapper. Letters spelling *Happy Easter.* This one surely deserved the longest life.

'Sweet Jesus,' Mammy declared. 'Seven chocolate eggs? It's a sin. You'd better be sharing them, my girl.'

It was no fault of mine there were so many. Number four – *with the speckly chocolate buttons* – was a gift from Mammy and Daddy and the rest from the Six Uncles, and the three biggest eggs given to me by the Unmarried Boys. Spoiled I was by Mammy's brothers, me being the only girl. At weekends they tipped pennies from their pockets for my savings. (Mine was the first hoola-hoop on the street.)

'Nothing better to spend their money on, I shouldn't wonder,' Daddy had said, catching the conversation in the kitchen where Mammy was at the stove and I was washing up her baking bowl, the wooden spoon already clean from my licking. He'd come in from his digging while Mammy was scolding.

'And a girl spoiled by handsome young men can come to no good,' she said.

Daddy wagged his finger at me but winked all the same. In his soil-crusty hands were three broken-stemmed daffodils the March wind had flattened.

'Soon, there'll be tulips out there,' he'd said, planting the rescued flowers in an empty milk bottle. Mammy had turned from her cooking.

'Soon, my man, your daughter will be totally ruined. You're as bad as the brothers.'

It was my childhood habit to say evening prayers kneeling, and all the while clutching my Great Grandpa's rosary, given to me shortly after his passing. Mammy had warned me never to lose it – though she said it was not necessary to hold on quite so tightly. Even so, I slept with it in my hand, believing it held us safe, the world turning, the stars in place. But when I'd woken that Easter morning my fingers were uncurled and empty, the rosary lost. I searched beneath the pillow, at the bottom of the bed, and as far under the mattress as my small hands could reach, but I didn't find it. Surely bad things would follow, so I tried to forget: counting eggs fifty times, counting one hundred; gorging and ticking their names from the list.
Until the day Jesus reminded me.

By the time of Our Lord's Visitation Easter was gone – along with six eggs, two each week. At least Jesus might watch over *the special one* left in my bedroom – though I knew in my heart that *Saviour of Chocolate* was unlikely His purpose.

On Tuesday and Wednesday sunshine prevailed, gifting our cheeks a fair smattering of freckles as we jumped over fallen logs, hopped around our scuffed leather satchels, hid behind hedges in the junior school yard. Jesus had sneaked summer in when we least expected. It seemed undeserved so early in the year, so at odds with the hush in our street and the curtains closed. I wondered if my chocolate egg was beading and sweating in its peep-through wrapper or had melted completely in such untimely heat, the flowers sunk into the shell, the letters spoiled.

On Thursday evening, I dropped my skates in the garden and dared to knock at my own front door. My heart beat in my throat. It was Mammy who answered. Her eyes were red and swollen and she wiped them on the hem of her checked cotton apron. She took hold of my arm and tugged, coaxing me over the doorstep.

'Come in,' she said. 'Come in and see your Daddy.'

'I've only come for my egg,' I said, pulling away, trembling at the thought of the white robes on the stairs.

She told me I should see Daddy in his frilly lace shirt front and I thought how he hated the bother of dressing up. She said he was fast asleep in my own little room and not to be afraid, and I said I wouldn't come in today – thank you. I peeked to one side of her, into the hall. On the cracked brown linoleum lay a bouquet of white lilies, and I wondered who'd grow blue flowers now for my May procession posy.

'It was all my fault,' I told Father Keenan at Saturday confession. 'Me eating those six whole eggs and losing Great Grandpa's rosary. And I saw Jesus on the stairs, Father. He knows what I did all right.'

'No, no,' Father said. 'You have it all wrong. Has nobody told you, child, that your daddy's heart was never much of a ticker? It'll be a hankie you'll be wanting there, Mary.'

When Daddy read his bed-time stories, my head snug upon his chest, I had listened for the thudding and the swishing of his heart, heard the stopping and the starting like holding a breath. And I'd held my breath too, counting those uneven, hop-skippy, hard to catch beats.

On Sunday Auntie told me I could go home to stay. I slept with Mammy and climbed the stairs only when she did, though Daddy had gone and there was no sign of Jesus on the landing. Mammy handed me the turquoise box and I lifted the lid and the egg with the Lily of the Valley was still there, sitting proud of its yellow satin bed. Though I had no words then to give voice to my certainty, I knew there'd be no more reindeer across a midnight sky.

On Monday after school I took the egg outside into

75

the garden. Around the lawn, a belt of blood-red tulips bowed their heads over the shrivelled daffodils, and I noticed my roller skates nestling among drooping leaves. I rested the box on the stone wall, opened the lid, tore off the orange wrapper.

'What do you have there?' called my pal, Mairead, from across the way, and she skipped towards me, all white bobby socks, and a blue stripy dirndl skirt like a summer parasol.

I stood for a moment stroking the satin and wondering: what was the colour of my Daddy's box lining? Was it white or blue or crinkled orange, frilly as his shirt front or plain as he'd have wished?

'Ah, it's nothing,' I said, picking up one skate. 'Just my last Easter egg. We can share it.'

Clasping the cold metal sole, I tapped the wheels on that fancy last egg, until the white lilies crumbled and the chocolate shell caved in like the soil on the edge of a hole in the ground, freshly dug.

Kirsty Fisher
Franko and the Fishheads
Children's fiction – novel extract

Chapter 1

Ten-year-old Frank Scales had never been chased across the beach by a seashell before, and he didn't much care for it. After wading through two rock pools, slipping on an abandoned tray of cheesy chips and squelching across a decaying jellyfish, he still hadn't managed to outrun it. Frank feared it might be an undiscovered deadly species of hermit crab that could travel at immense speed. Perhaps he had accidentally trampled on a member of its family and it was coming to get revenge?

'Argghhhh!' he groaned after glancing backwards to see the shell just a few metres behind him. 'I don't want to have to hurt you, crab!' he called out. 'Don't come any closer!'

As Frank was fast approaching the cliffs, he knew he had little choice. He turned around to face the shell and decided he would try to kick it, not to cause the crab any pain of course – just to make sure it ended up as far in the opposite direction as possible. But Frank's leg swung against thin air, and his body jerked awkwardly before he fell onto the sand. Unhurt but humiliated, he jumped up and glanced around to check that nobody had seen.

They hadn't. The beach was empty as was usual for 8pm on a Sunday evening. And even better, the shell seemed to have disappeared. Frank laughed nervously to himself and decided that the best thing would be to go home immediately before anything else weird happened.

But it was too late. Before he had even taken his first step, the sand around his feet started to shake and the shell burrowed out from beneath it. After flipping over, not to reveal a new species of hermit crab but a spiralling, shadowy emptiness, Frank heard for the first time the whispered word that would change his life forever:

'Fraaaaaaaaaaaaankooooooooo!'

He knelt down, knowing that what he was about to do was probably a bad idea. For some reason he just couldn't help himself. Frank picked the shell up, then placed it to his ear.

He heard the familiar echoing sound of the sea from within, like the waves as they lapped up the beach. It sounded far away at first, but then it got closer and closer, as if the tide was coming in. There was also a sound that Frank didn't recognise, a strange hissing that was getting louder. He pressed the shell to his ear as hard as he could and tried to make it out, then he froze as the hiss turned into the very same whisper he had heard just a moment ago:

'When the eight-legged-mini-men roam around free,
we'll meet by the death stones facing the sea. . .'

Frank shook the shell as hard as he could, and felt sure he was going mad as the hiss-turned-whisper changed again, this time into a low pitched, slobbery demand:

'DON'T BE LATE FRANKO!'

At this point, Frank didn't hesitate. He threw the shell into the air then booted it with all his might.

It disappeared and this time it didn't come back.

Chapter 2

'Home Mum!' Frank yelled as he slammed the front door of the little seaside bungalow where he lived. 'Something really weird just happened!'

Frank's mum hummed and carried on cleaning.

She had been cleaning a lot recently, especially late at night. Frank's grandma said it was because this time ten years ago his good-for-nothing-lay-about-father up and left without giving them any explanation. She said his mum was trying to occupy herself so that she didn't have to think about it.

Frank thought this was very strange. If he was trying to occupy himself he watched TV, or played on the Xbox that Mrs Speight had given him when Kieran had an upgrade, or he went to his favourite place ever (the beach) to explore, like he had been doing for the last three hours. Cleaning was not something he would ever choose to do, that was for sure.

'So, what's this weird thing that happened then?' Frank's mum said as she put down her duster and poured herself a glass of wine. 'Did Kieran see it too?'

Whoops. Frank realised he had dropped himself in trouble. He was supposed to have been to the beach with Kieran Speight, his horrible next door neighbour. But as Kieran enjoyed nothing more than pushing Frank into rock-pools and rubbing seaweed in his face, Frank had never called for him.

'Erm,' Frank said as he backed off in the direction of his room, 'yeah. I'm going to go to bed. Night Mum!'

Frank's mum looked at him suspiciously, then walked over.

'I hope you two aren't up to anything,' she said with a chuckle as she ruffled Frank's hair.

Frank forced a smile. He knew his mum liked to think he and Kieran were best of friends, but in reality they didn't get on one bit. Frank never said anything though, it was easier this way.

'Go on then, off to bed' his mum went on. 'I am doing the early shift at the fish factory tomorrow. I'll leave your breakfast on the table.'

Frank nodded as his mum dashed off to reposition the photo frames on either side of the mantelpiece (they were not quite at symmetrical angles). Frank went to his room and got ready for bed.

Chapter 3

It was 11.15 when Frank woke from a dream he couldn't quite remember. The words 'Don't be late Fraaaankooo' were running through his head and he had an overwhelming urge to go outside.

After about half an hour of tossing and turning he jumped out of bed and shoved his trainers on. He knew that he had school the next day, but guessed it didn't really make any difference if he couldn't sleep anyway. So after forcing the bedroom window open, Frank tumbled out onto the street below.

'Urgghhhh!' he groaned as he realised he had accidentally trodden on something crunchy. He lifted up his foot. The squished body of a spider and its remaining legs were twitching on the bottom of his shoe.

'Eight-legged-mini-men...' Frank muttered curiously to himself as he looked up and noticed there were many more spiders crawling on the steps that led all the way to the cliff-top graveyard. Hoping it was just a coincidence and nothing whatsoever to do with the bizarre message in the shell, he began walking up them. His stomach lurched as the outline of the ancient gravestones ahead came into view, but strangely, he couldn't bring himself to turn back.

'Ello Franko.'

Frank heard the voice he had been dreading the moment he reached the top step. Like before it was low pitched and slobbery, but this time it sounded more ridiculous than scary. Frank figured that nothing so ridiculous could really be evil, and he burst out laughing.

'Whhhy do you laugh, Frankoooo?'

A stranger cloaked in a seaweed-matted net appeared from behind a particularly old and decrepit gravestone.

'Erm, I don't know...' Frank replied, trying not to

sound too shocked or rude. 'I remembered a good joke,' he lied.

The stranger took a step closer.

'Now is not the time for jokes, Frankooo,' he replied.

As Frank stared he noticed a pair of huge, gormless, boggly eyes rolling around beneath the cloak's hood. They looked quite funny and he spluttered his reply:

'Why are you calling me Franko when my name is Fra...'

The stranger lunged forward and clamped something slimy and wet over Frank's mouth, glanced to the left, then to the right, and whispered before Frank had a chance to finish.

'Shhhhh! Do not mention that name again, Franko do you hear!'

Frank wiped a coating of prawn-puree-scented saliva from his hair and face and wiped it on his trousers as discreetly as possible. The stranger released his grip, then took a swig from an ancient flask and gargled. The whole time he kept his boggly eyes fixed on Frank.

'The Fishheads are looking for you, so I call you Franko for your own protection, and for reasons of SSS. As Franko, you are safe.'

Frank frowned.

'What on earth is SSS?' he asked.

The stranger tutted impatiently.

'It has nothing to do with earth, Franko,' he replied. 'Only the sea. SSS means Seven Seas Security.'

Frank kept frowning.

'Right' he replied. 'So my safety, and the security of the seven seas, depends on an O?'

The stranger clapped loudly and smiled.

'Yes Franko – it's genius!'

His shiny protruding lips glistened under the moonlight, and he didn't appear to have any teeth underneath them, which explained why his smile was abnormally wide and slobbery. Before Frank really had a chance to look properly the smile vanished and he began whispering again.

'If...if...the Fishheads hear me calling you by your real name they will find you and flapperghast you to death. Franko is a top secret code name. You will be safer, because the Fishheads will never guess you are...'

He paused, moved closer, winked at Frank with a boggly eye and mouthed 'Frank.'

Frank smiled uneasily. He was certain that this being was both the simplest and ugliest he had ever met. Living in Britley, he knew that was really saying something.

'So what...what is flapperghasting?' he asked nervously.

The stranger rolled his boggly eyes as if Frank's question had a very obvious answer.

'The opposite of flipperghasting of course!' he chuckled.

'Okaaaaay. . .' Frank said, not daring to admit he didn't know what that was either. 'And why are these Fishheads looking for me?'

The stranger's smile turned into a frown.

'Because of what your father did,' he whispered. 'And because you are the Lost Manphibian.'

Frank pulled a face.

'What's my dad got to do with anything?' he replied. 'He disappeared before I was born and I never heard from him since.'

After shuffling around awkwardly for a moment the stranger made a bizarre, embarrassed sort of bubbling noise. It was pretty disgusting so Frank took a little step back.

As the church bells started to chime the stranger stumbled backwards against a gravestone. Then with a startled look in his eyes he began pacing toward the cliff edge, pulling his thick, net-covered cloak behind him as if it were light as silk.

'No time to lose Franko!' he called back

breathlessly. 'You must wait until I send you another message via a Secret Shell.'

'But I have more questions!' Frank shrieked as he jogged behind. 'Like how do you know about my dad? And what. . . what are Fishheads...?'

The stranger's mouth stretched into a smile. Then he raised his cloak toward the moonshine.

His mouth was bob-bobbing like a fish.

His eyes were outward-popping like a fish.

His hands, which were stretched out wide, were not hands at all but a pair of fins (like a fish).

'Arrrggghhhhhh!' Frank yelled as the clock struck twelve.

'YOU are a Fishhead!'

The figure nodded his slimy goldfish head.

'The only one who can help you, Franko.'

Then he walked backwards with surprising grace to the cliff edge and back-flipped into the sea.

Frank stood back from the top and gawped. He realised when it was too late that there was still one question that remained unanswered.

'What's a Manphibian?' he muttered to himself.

Suzannah Evans

He found his brother in the penguin enclosure

at London Zoo. Last year's nestling, fuzz-crested,
he popped into the rucksack with no fuss
and stayed there, one eye to a rivet hole.
Why did you leave me here? he whispered.
Their parents were far ahead;
it was feeding time at the giant tortoise
who chewed lettuce with leathery, slow-motion jaws.
Mum said *Doesn't it look like Grandad*
and the boy thought his whole family might be here,
each with their own chain-link fence.

At home he'd often find him in the bath,
floating on his belly, adding cold from the tap.
I'm hot, he'd say, a plate of fish-fingers
soggy on the mat. When the snow days came
he played out longer than any kid on the street,
lost all of their scarves, refused his bedtime.
As the light died on the garden he'd thump snowballs
against the front window where his family stood
in silhouette, glad to be out of the draught.

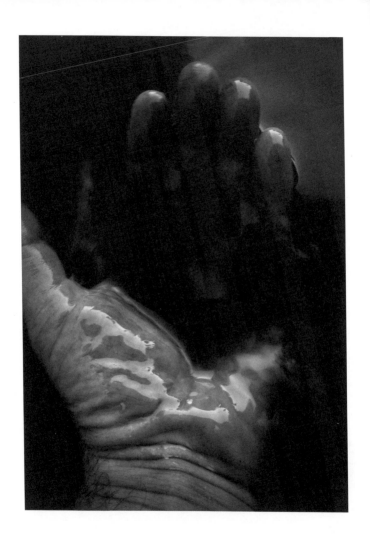

David Devanny
the people of the light

we are
i'm quite sure
the morlocks

and we have come to eat you

    today
of all days
was the time to manicure
your fine hands

you want to go out
with a bang
don't you?

and they will look great
when you are
    gripping
my grubby flaxen hair

oh yeah

we are the morlocks
and we have come to eat you

and i do hope
you played in the sun
light in the water
falls and danced today

because we are the morlocks
we have risen from the ground
we have come with the night
and we have come to eat you

Andy Koller
Waiting for Cancer

A MAN stands on stage smoking the end of a cigarette.
He takes his last drag and drops it on the floor, then stamps it with
his foot. He looks around, bored. He looks at his watch and then
lights another. He takes a long drag, and exhales slowly, clearly
enjoying it. He winces in pain and looks down at his foot. He
takes his shoe off and checks it for stones... nothing. He looks
confused, then dismisses it and puts his shoe back on. Throughout
the scene he occasionally looks at his foot and winces
uncomfortably.

A WOMAN enters and stands next to him. He acknowledges her
with a nod and then returns to his moment of bliss. She puts a
cigarette to her lips, lights it and then exhales in the same manner
as him. They stand for a moment in their own contemplative
silences, then...

WOMAN:	So how's it going?
MAN:	All right I guess. I hate Mondays. There's always so much to do. I didn't get any chance to do anything over the weekend. They always come and go so quickly. It's like you've barely had time to scratch before Friday night turns into Monday morning. *Pause.*
WOMAN:	I meant with the quitting. *She nods at the cigarette.*
MAN:	Oh, that. Yeah, all right I suppose. *He takes another long drag and exhales.*
WOMAN:	It's just that... you're...
MAN:	What? *Pause – the Woman nods towards his cigarette. He nods back in acknowledgment.*
WOMAN:	That's why I wondered...

MAN:	Hmm.
WOMAN:	How it was going…
MAN:	*(shrugs)* It's going well.
WOMAN:	But you're still smoking.
MAN:	Yeah. How's your quitting?
WOMAN:	How do you think?
	She holds up her cigarette.
MAN:	It looks like you're doing fine.
	Pause.
WOMAN:	Are you being awkward on purpose?
MAN:	I'm not being awkward.
WOMAN:	Yes you are. How can you say your quitting is going well when you're stood there smoking?
MAN:	It's a long story.
	Pause.
WOMAN:	Well?
MAN:	What?
WOMAN:	Come on… I want to know.
MAN:	The story?
WOMAN:	Yes!
MAN:	It's not very interesting.
WOMAN:	I'll decide that.
MAN:	It's long and it doesn't really go anywhere.
WOMAN:	Just like this exchange.
MAN:	But you'll be bored. I don't want to bore you.
WOMAN:	I asked, didn't I?
MAN:	I suppose.
WOMAN:	Come on, it's become a 'thing' now. I need to know. Anyway, what's wrong with being bored? Everyone gets bored. It's the great leveller. In a way, boredom is what the human condition is really about. That and death. We will be bored, and we will die. Nothing else is certain.
MAN:	You're starting to bore me now.
WOMAN:	See? Now you owe me.
MAN:	Well, OK, I'll bore you. What was it again?
WOMAN:	Smoking.

MAN:	Oh yeah, well a while ago I pretty much stopped smoking almost by accident. Without realising it, I was smoking less and less in a day. It annoyed me. I really like smoking, and so I decided to do something about it.
	He lights another.
WOMAN:	So, you decided to quit smoking in order to start smoking again.
MAN:	Precisely. Every time I've actively tried to quit, I've ended up smoking more because I was constantly thinking about it.
WOMAN:	So actively trying to quit leads to smoking more, which you want to achieve because you enjoy it…
MAN:	Exactly. So when you ask how the quitting is going, and I say 'pretty well', it really is because I'm doing what I set out to do.
	Pause. I told you it'd be boring.
WOMAN:	No, I'm not bored, you're just an idiot.
MAN:	But I'm back up to forty a day… or not.
	Pause. The Woman lights another cigarette.
MAN:	*(noticing)* You seem to be doing well 'n' all.
WOMAN:	I'm actually trying to quit, as in… you know… stopping smoking.
MAN:	You're probably not doing very well then.
	She nods.
WOMAN:	I was doing well. I was down to one a day, after dinner in the evening.
MAN:	What happened?
WOMAN:	I was talking to someone about how I used to smoke. How much I enjoyed it, how it seemed that everything I did was punctuated by a cigarette, you know?
	He nods and inhales.
WOMAN:	Get up, have a cigarette. Get dressed, have a cigarette. Go to work, have a cigarette.
MAN:	Like a nicotine full-stop to every important

	moment in a day.
WOMAN:	Yeah…
MAN:	So, what happened?
WOMAN:	This woman I was talking to just started crying about how I shouldn't smoke because she'd just lost her father to lung cancer, and how it'll get me one day.

Pause.

MAN:	That's horrible.
WOMAN:	I know. I needed a cigarette to calm down. Well, the floodgates opened. I went on a huge smoking binge. My lungs were like Pompeii for three days… pipes, cigars, cigarettes, patches, Nicorette gum… you name it, I smoked it.
MAN:	You smoked patches and gum?
WOMAN:	*(embarrassed)* Yeah.

Pause.

MAN:	How?
WOMAN:	Don't ask. Anyway, the upshot of it is I'm back where I started.

Without looking he offers her his pack. She takes one and lights it.

MAN:	I hate when people bang on about cancer and banning smoking.
WOMAN:	It's a form of bullying. Don't they realise we're addicts? We need sympathy.

Pause.

MAN:	I mean… I have a physical reaction whenever I see children. I break out in a cold sweat, I start shaking and panicking.
WOMAN:	Stress.
MAN:	Stress. Children make me ill. It starts with the stress, which can lead to heart conditions, which can lead to cancer.
WOMAN:	Stress doesn't cause cancer.
MAN:	It's true. Stress can be a direct route to cancer. I researched it on Wikipedia and everything. You know what it means though,

	don't you?
WOMAN:	What.
MAN:	In a certain light, children are carcinogenic. But do we ban them? Oh, no. It's a massive double standard if you ask me.
WOMAN:	But by that rationale we should ban burnt toast.
MAN:	A little Samuel Beckett play, each and every one.
WOMAN:	Eh?
MAN:	*(child and adult voice)* 'I want chocolate.' 'No, have a carrot, it's better for you.' 'But I want chocolate.' 'Have a carrot.' 'I want chocolate.' 'No!' 'Chocolate!' 'Oh for God's sake, fine, here. Have the bloody chocolate.' 'But I've got earache.' *Pause - she's realised something.*
WOMAN:	That's why you smoke isn't it? The stress caused by children is alleviated by cigarettes.
MAN:	No, it's why I teach. If I had a job I believed in or enjoyed in any way, the cigarettes wouldn't be half as important as they are.
WOMAN:	But children are the future.
MAN:	Only if you believe that time is linear. *They simultaneously check their watches, extinguish cigarettes.*
MAN:	What you got now?
WOMAN:	Free period. You?
MAN:	My year 7s.
WOMAN:	What you doing with them?
MAN:	We're looking at the concept of metaphysical determinism.
WOMAN:	That sounds heavy.
MAN:	It certainly is.
WOMAN:	But they're year 7s. They'll get bored and start messing about. That'll wind you up. *Man holds his cigarette packet up.*
MAN	I know.

THE END

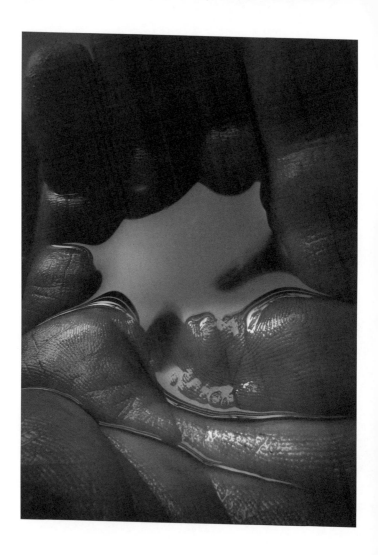

Suzanne McArdle
Isobars

In the barometer of his knees and hips
approaching rain sets up a throb.
He turns his cheek to Cairo and Baghdad
where the sun always shone, and he dipped
into bars, found mint tea, dancing and opium.
Swallows flit between Africa and Blighty,
flying up the Nile over unknown countries,
yet somehow returning to the same gardens.

Now he circumnavigates in shrinking isobars
to doctor, dentist, and optician. The earth cracks in Africa.
He closes the curtains, battens hatches like a submariner;
still sunlight beams a line of fade along the sofa,
and water pushes through the leaky guttering.
The radio forecasts gales in Cromarty, Forties and Viking.

Matthew Rhodes
The Squirrel Enthusiast's Office

'NO. NO. I need to cancel a standing order. I NEED this doing today. Am I speaking English? Just cancel my standing order!'

'B-B-But Mr Schloss, I need to follow standard security procedures. All I require are the first and third digits from your online banking pin number and then I would be able to cancel your standing order for you. Do you understand?' asked Toby, whilst adjusting his headset.

'I've never heard so much rubbish in my life! I've already told you about ten times, I do not have an online banking pin number, so how can I give you that information? Look, I work for a very important business!'

'But Mr Schloss, it says here on my system that you are fully enrolled for online banking, so that means you definitely have a pin number. I'm sorry if this is causing some distress.'

Silence. Maybe Mr Schloss had finally calmed down a little.

'You're an absolute idiot aren't you? What is your name?'

'Toby Woolston.'

He winced as soon as he said that. You were only meant to reveal your first name to the customer. It could be considered a breach of security if you gave your full name. In the grand scheme of things it really shouldn't matter too much though.

'I hate people like you. Do you get satisfaction from telling people you can't do things for them? You people will get some sort of comeuppance. I shan't be wasting my breath on you any longer.'

Mr Schloss put the phone down. Toby stared

blankly at his computer screen. It was five fifty-eight. Time for one more call. A beep came through on his headset. He quickly checked a man called Edward Jenkins through security.

'You're speaking to Toby, may I help?'

'Well…I hope you can. I've got this new card and it's really confusing me. Can you shed any light on this?'

'Certainly, Mr Jenkins. From what I can see here on the system, you reported your card stolen last week and so you've been sent a replacement card. Your account is not affected in the slightest, so there's no need to worry.'

'Oh no, I understand that, I'm not thick. What's confusing me is that this new card has a different number on the front from all my other cards.'

'Well, every card has its own number at the front. It's called a PAN number and every card has a different one. So just to assure you, there's nothing to worry about there!'

'I'm sorry, are you new at this job or something?'

'No, Mr Jenkins, I've worked here for some time now.'

'Then you must realise that what you are saying is completely wrong.'

Toby shook his head and looked at everyone sitting on his row. Everyone unified by boredom and stress. He could see thin strips of sunlight shining through the gaps in the blinds at the window. This only made him more agitated.

'I can assure you that every debit card has its own unique long card number at the front. That's why your new card has a different number from your previous one. Your account won't be affected in the slightest.'

'How old are you? You sound as if you're just going through puberty?'

'I'm twenty-six.'

'Well I'm eighty-two years old and I didn't reach this age by being a brainless oaf. I've been around a lot longer than you, so I actually know what I'm talking about. Right, LISTEN to me when I tell you this. I've been banking with you for over sixty years now and my cards have always had the same number apart from this new one. So I want you to order me a replacement card that has the same long number on it that I've had for the past fifteen years.'

'I wouldn't be able to do that I'm afraid.'

'I have all my debit cards since I've been banking with you right in front of me. And lo and behold, they all have the same long number at the front. I can show you now on Skype if you want?'

Toby would have preferred to be living in a two bedroom apartment with the Devil than continue talking to this clown. He just wanted to be sitting in his pretty garden. With a cup of tea and biscuits.

'I can't use Skype with you at a banking call centre, Mr Jenkins.'

'Are you a ninny?'

'Sorry.'

'I said, are you a ninny? Because I think you are one.'

'Mr Jenkins, can I...'

'Will you stop saying my name all the time! Are you or are you not a ninny? Answer me!'

'Mr Je- I can confirm to you that I am not a ninny.'

'Well, I think you are. Goodbye.'

The line went dead and Toby leaned back on his chair and sighed.

Toby arrived back at his house an hour later and began walking up the stairs. It was not until he reached the fifth floor that he deduced something wasn't quite right. Mainly, that his house, to his knowledge, had only ever had three floors. He went up another flight just out of curiosity; sure enough, another floor containing two rooms and another flight of stairs upwards. He did the same thing again resulting in the same outcome. Cautiously, he knocked on one of the doors. No answer. He turned the handle slowly but the door was locked. How do you explain this to the estate agents, he wondered? He continued the process of knocking and trying the doors before walking up yet another set of stairs.

By his reckoning, it was on the seventeenth floor that he noticed an official-looking sign on one of the doors. It read:

Mr Bob Winter
Floor 17
Recruitment Consultant

He knocked tentatively.

'Come in!' said a jolly voice from inside.

Toby opened the door very slowly. A man in a suit was sitting at a desk with a computer in front of him as well as several forms and documents.

'Ah, Mr Woolston, you're here nice and early, excellent! Do take a seat, young man!'

Toby sat down in front of him as instructed. He looked at the walls around the room and at the framed photograph next to his computer. The photo was of a squirrel. In fact, all the walls in the room had pictures of squirrels. His house had been taken over by a serial squirrel enthusiast. This was all he needed.

'Well, I'll just quickly introduce myself. My name's Bob Winter and I'm the recruitment consultant here and I understand you want to be a professional gardener. Is that right?'

'H-How did you know that? More to the point, why are you in my house? There wasn't a seventeenth floor when I walked out the door this morning!'

Bob chuckled to himself and kept playing with his giant greying beard with his hand.

'Don't fret, Mr Woolston! All will be explained in due course. In fact, I've been tracking your progress for some time. I know how much you want to be a professional gardener because that's what makes you happy and that's how you like to express yourself. You've always felt that there's something special about working in the open air, haven't you?'

'Yes...yes I have.'

'And I can see just from looking into your eyes now that you're broken. You're terrified, aren't you, of doing the same terrible job year after year and wasting all your potential? You're scared that you're letting your family down and that all your friends will eventually drift away from you when they move onto bigger and better things. And I can see all that just from looking into those eyes of yours,' concluded Bob, still playing with his beard.

'What do you actually do?' asked Toby, his voice shaking a little.

'I work for *Good Fortune*. See, it does actually exist. You've been one of my case studies for a while now actually. You weren't scheduled for good fortune for another year, around April time, but I've had a word with one of my superiors and I've arranged an interview for you with one of our team leaders on floor thirty to see if you can be considered eligible now rather than next year.'

'And I'll be a professional gardener? Never have to do any other job anymore? How is this even happening?' Toby asked.

'Well, technically you're unconscious. Well, not exactly unconscious, but we've sort of paused your real self. I won't bore you with the details, it's not really interesting or fascinating in the slightest. Once this interview has been completed, we'll put you back to your normal self and this change of fortune will take place over the next few days, but you'll have been tuned so that it still comes as a welcome surprise and turn of events for you. That's how *Good Fortune* works. You just have to sign the contract at the end of the interview.'

'And it's on floor 30? The guy I need to see now?'

Bob nodded with a warm smile. Toby practically skipped out of the door. Just before he departed the room though, he had to ask one final question.

'Why are there loads of pictures of squirrels in this office?'

Bob chuckled.

'I just bloody love squirrels. Seriously, when have you ever seen a cheeky little squirrel and not felt a bit better about everything? It's our symbol for *Good Fortune*.'

Toby decided not to pursue this enquiry, thanked him, closed the office door and virtually flew up the remaining flights to get to the room where he could sign the contract. He felt as if all his Christmas mornings had rolled into one moment.

When Toby reached the office door at floor 30, he read:

Hermann Schloss
Head of Good Fortune Approval

He knocked.

'Come in!' shouted a voice.

In stepped Toby, his whole body trembling.

'Ah, today is your lucky day! You've got nothing to worry about in this interview, Mr Woolston. Or, Toby Woolston I should say.' Mr Schloss looked Toby dead in the eye. 'Now, now, hang on a minute. Where have I heard that name before? Oh yes, I remember…see, I could tell it was you just from looking into those eyes of yours. Well…I trust you have your pin number at hand,' said Mr Schloss.

'W-What pin number?'

'Your Good Fortune pin number, Mr Woolston. It says here on my system that you definitely have a pin number for our service. It's a standard security procedure, Mr Woolston, do you understand?'

'But I was never issued with any pin number. Can you not put me through security another way?'

'I'm sorry, but if you cannot confirm your pin details, then you cannot sign my lovely contract here and I will be unable to help you. In which case, I shall have to hang up on you.'

And as soon as Mr Schloss said that, the pause was taken off and Toby returned to his normal self.

Nine o'clock in the morning. Headset on. The same glum expression etched on everyone's face.

'You're speaking to Toby, may I help?'

He slumped back on his chair and looked out of the window. He saw a squirrel foraging for nuts.

Joanne Ailward-Irwin
I Saw You Climb

I saw you climb once
air-bound
straining
edging
geo-angled
pinching rock   gecko-like

chalk-tipped
perched rubber-toed

at the top you sang   see me

clouds churning under the 'O' sun
tearing the rock face
in cracks
compacted   histories
grit   frowning granite
limestone

into   fissures
hard   syllables
driving spikes

the bull rock   bucked you   from its back
breaking
parts of   you
the
heated   innards   of   mountain hearts

bound us   encircling fingers

why climb I asked   I love mountains you said

Mark Thorpe
Cold Breath of Summer

Novel extract

I had to give Frankie her due. The Chocolate Orange was a lovely touch. She'd bought it for me as the supplementary Christmas present only a few days earlier. Now I found it exploded like a dirty bomb on top of the pile of my good clothes outside the house. She'd dumped them like charity discards between two parked cars whilst I'd been out overnight. All around were boxes of books, DVDs and the smashed remains of my Xbox extending under the tail of Gordon's Nissan. This time there'd be hell to pay. Parking in the street was difficult enough as it was.

I picked out some clean pants and a T-shirt, went in, had a shower.

Luckily I'd bought in a good area with the proceeds from my TV series. I'd moved up in the world from window-licker to curtain-twitcher. Bought outright as well, although Frankie would be sure to want half.

I peered out of the front door following my sluice and smiled into the CCTV camera stationed below the gable, knowing it would keep a watchful eye on the street for another couple of minutes. I went in and scanned the footage. I felt a strange sense of pride that Frankie's good looks weren't totally dependent on the efforts of her hairdresser, beautician and personal shopper. Olive skin and good cheekbones would take her far in this life. There was ten minutes of fury, exhibiting all the passion that she brought to our rows, then her back to me as she stomped out of my life, with her Mulberry holdall and the flight case with the wonky wheel.

Perhaps it would have been different if I'd texted.

Itchy feet kept taking me back to my old haunts, trying to spark some new material into life, without success. I needed some grit in the oyster for that to happen, not comfy domesticity. Happiness was still proving elusive. Before I left her last night, I'd sellotaped a load of biscuits to her white Audi, thinking it might make her laugh. It obviously didn't.

I went back into the street and started collecting up the clothes. There was some good stuff there. Frankie had helped pick them out for me, overhauling my look once the money had started pouring in. Collarless shirts, waistcoats, establishing that Americana frontiersman look rather than the plaid shirt and jeans grunge style I'd had since being a teenager. At least she hadn't ripped things to pieces. All of it was salvageable.

'Hello Chris.'

I looked up. It was Gordon's wife, Carla. She'd obviously been checking for my return.

'Hi Carla. Sorry about this,' I said, brushing my hands as I rose from the tarmac.

'No, don't. She gone fe good, you know?'

'I guessed that might be the case.' I looked at her blankly, trying to feel which emotion was going to well up uncontrollably.

Carla must have mistaken this for contrition, as she moved forward and enveloped me in her warm West Indian bosom.

I sniffed and she released me, adjusted her glasses, held me at arm's length.

'She was at ours for tea and chat till gone two last night, you know.'

'Did you sit up with her? You shouldn't have, you know. She'll list my faults to any passing stranger.'

'I do feel sorry for the girl.'

'You can't believe everything she says, Carla,' I said resignedly. I'd not had time to dry my hair and it lay long, lank and flat, itching with the frost.

'I know she can be a difficult woman at times, Chris, but she deserve better than this.'

I thought that Frankie had done alright out of me. It was never going to be one of those relationships that was meant to last. She was only presenting on Children's TV when we started out.

'What did she tell you, then?'

I picked up a battered cardboard box full of books. Frankie had known these were special to me; they were the ones that I'd received in my Granddad William's will. She'd better not have ruined them. Granddad had always treated them with such care, protective of the knowledge they held. Not that there was much there for the connoisseur or collector. *The Field Guide to Birds*, an atlas, *The Old Holborn Book of Boxing*, and a set of alphabetised encyclopedias. Just enough to help him make sense of the world. He'd grown up and lived on the east coast. Made his living on fishing boats. Probably went as far as Holland, Grimsby, and Scotland and that was about it.

'D'y'wanna finish putting them things away, and pop over? I'll make a cup a tea.' Carla smiled, hesitated, awaiting a reply.

Course you want to get my side, I thought, suddenly disgruntled, just to check that everything Frankie said was true.

'Okay,' I said, desperately wondering whether it would be worth bluffing it out one last time that it wasn't my fault. 'But I need to see my agent first. Another of his crisis meetings.'

I arrived at Alex's office slightly behind schedule. He raised an eyebrow archly as I came in.

'What time do you call this?'

'Roughly late.'

Alex smiled, obviously remembering that he needed to indulge the Talent.

'Come on in, sit down, don't worry.'

I was thinking of how many of these planning meetings we'd had since the tour finished. 180,000 tickets at £24 apiece. Alex would send me out there for another five months the moment he had the chance, and if I were him, I'd send me too. But where was the fun in that? I'd wrung every last second of excitement I could from that experience. I knew that I'd end up just like the others – writing the same old gags, using the same received wisdom to create the same knee-jerk laughs. Worse than those poor sods from the old days who played summer season and working men's clubs with the same old act every night for years on end, trusting that the audience had never heard it before. I had been glazing over as Alex was speaking.

'I'm getting rather concerned that you're limiting your options. Can't tour, can't go back to radio. You need to get some exposure. Not too much, 'cos we haven't got the material, but not too little, 'cos I can see this as being a big six months for you, Chrissy Boy.'

'I want to do the legalise heroin piece on TV,' I said.

'It's not TV, Chris. That's stand-up. Maybe the first couple of lines on the trailer for the next DVD. We could do it on a panel show.'

'I don't want to do panel shows.'

'What then?' Alex continued to probe.

'What about if we get on somewhere where they're not expecting me to be funny?' I said instinctively.

'What do you mean?' he asked.

'It would be funny on Question Time.'

'Ha Ha. That would be committing career suicide. You as a panelist on Question Time. You know nothing about politics,' said Alex.

'Get me in the audience then. I'll do it from there!' I said triumphantly, thinking at last I'd thought of something original. I didn't see the blind alley he was cornering me in.

'I've got you a DIY makeover show. But with a twist. They want to do it live.'

He paused just to give this dramatic statement even more gravitas than I thought could ever be possible for a failed graduate from the Liverpool School of Performing Arts.

'Can you picture it? You presenting, keeping it bubbling. They were very interested in your ability to make things happen on screen. In fact, you were in the top two when it was green-lit.'

'I'm touched,' I said. 'Right up there in the top two, eh? Who turned it down?'

'It doesn't matter about that. It means it's all ready to go. Filming starts in two weeks. Bound to be a cult favourite with the students.'

I cut in, feigning enthusiasm, 'I'll do it.'

He looked at me as if I'd turned into someone else in front of his eyes. This would buy me enough breathing space, so that I could sort out my love life.

'That's great. Really great,' said Alex, giving me a bit of an awkward man-hug.

'Scripted or unscripted?' I asked.

'I'll ask for unscripted. You feel better making it up as you go along, yeah?'

When I got home I thawed out a little of the country vegetable soup I'd made from the Christmas leftovers, cheered by its homely smell.

The box of Granddad's books was still in the hallway. It no longer had its folding lips. Rips were appearing down its sides, revealing its corrugated veins. I'd not taken them out of that box since I got them – the container as important as the contents, just as he was only ash without the urn – but they now needed a better home.

I picked up the Field Guide, turned its comforting weight in my hands. The pages had a mustiness that transported me, made me realise I hadn't been to the countryside for years. I'd have to see what I could remember. I took the book through to the lounge, switching on the light as I went. I'd already sunk deep into an armchair and flicked it open, before the low-energy bulb had fully kicked in, making the pages look more aged than they actually were.

I smiled at the archaic tone of the introduction, with its Instructions for Proper Usage; the familial groupings: Divers and Grebes; Pelicans and Allies – I remembered having to ask Granddad what that word meant. The odd idea that groups of birds were at war together – Herons and Allies; Ducks, Geese and Swans; Rails and Allies; Gulls and Terns. Their shapes in silhouette against a sky of text. I flicked through the pages, entranced just by their names – Night Heron, Lapwing, Sandwich Tern.

Granddad knew them all, describing them by their actions as much as their looks. Even as he slowed down with age and hard work he had that stillness, gauging his surroundings, allowing events to unfold around him with the certainty of experience.

'Chris,' he'd whispered. 'Hold you hard, my boy. See that?'

I was back on marshland, ten or eleven years old, autumn was creeping. Granddad was pointing out towards the water's edge into the reeds. Bittern, their heads raised skyward, ochre yellow beaks like tweezers, sensing any changes in the salty air.

I turned the pages of the book, noting the tick and the date entry he'd made: 4th August 1990 – I was ten, not eleven.

We'd been out since first light. Nanny Rose silently working away making our sandwiches; Granddad had cheese and pickle, four slices, which he always insisted had to be wrapped in greaseproof paper; I would have had tuna in cellophane. We ate them in patches of lavender and gorse, sitting on Granddad's coat. When I started to feel the cold, we made a small fire.

'You trees,' he'd said as a Granddad joke, addressing the yew trees. 'You'll burn well.'

He'd let me hold some twigs in the fire, to see if they would catch. I watched with nervous excitement as they glowed red like sparklers, then dropped them into the fire once they had flared into colour. His big hand enveloped mine, lifting the flame upwards so that it didn't burn my fingers.

'Why don't we get Mum and Dad to come next time?' I suggested, not understanding why they didn't want to be here to enjoy this with me.

'They will one year,' said Granddad watching the

dusk chase the day away. 'Till then you've got me.'

I made some space on the bottom shelf. The Field Guide went in first, then the atlas, the boxing book, the encyclopedias last. There was something very strange about pre-Google knowledge. Someone had decided what was important enough to include. I got to the bottom of the box. Wi-Z. I took it in my right hand, squashing the shelved books together with my left hand to make space for it. A brown envelope slipped from inside the covers. I held it in my fingers. No stamps, no address, unsealed with the flap folded in. Three words written on it in capitals: 'THIS IS WHY'.

I looked inside. Black and white photos, the size of my palm. Three inches by four, with white borders. Dirty photos.

Michèle Roberts
Ghosts – an essay

I don't believe in ghosts. I do believe in ghosts. Perhaps in that crack of doubt, between belief and disbelief, the ghost can appear.

In 1991 I saw a ghost. No, not saw the image of a dead person so much as experienced a haunting. Early that year my aunt Brigitte died in her little brick cottage near Etretat in Normandy, where she lived alone. She was my godmother, a single, professional woman who had taught domestic science all her life. We were very close. I admired her independence and zest for life, enjoyed her fierceness, her sudden bursts of gaiety. She taught me to cook classic French dishes and took me on walking holidays in Burgundy. Once she became ill, I visited her more often than formerly, but was not with her when she died. My mother was. She telephoned me with the news and I jumped on the boat to Le Havre.

In accordance with local Catholic custom, the corpse was laid out in the house for three days so that everyone could come and pay their last respects. Brigitte's body lay in the little downstairs salon, which she had taken over as a bedroom once she fell ill, the room in which both my grandparents had died. When I went in to say goodbye to Brigitte, I was puzzled and frightened by her yellow, waxy face. She was both there and yet not there. That night I slept in her attic bedroom just overhead. I didn't like sleeping above a corpse, felt jumpy and unsettled. In the middle of the night I was startled by a knocking and gurgling in the wall. I sat up, terrified. The ancient central heating system had decided to turn itself on. Tap, tap, tap at the door; a whisper; the door creaking open. A vision in a pale robe. It was my mother, coming in to see whether I was all right. Perhaps she wanted comfort too.

After the funeral, after the wake, the little house stayed empty. My mother and her brother, the inheritors, hadn't yet decided whether to keep the house or sell it. A good neighbour, who had loved Brigitte, went in daily to open the shutters and windows and air the place. My mother knew I longed for a little French house with a garden (my husband Jim and I lived in a small top-floor flat in London), hoped that I might decide to buy Brigitte's house, encouraged me and Jim to go and stay there for a long weekend break. Off we went.

The house felt full of something electric, chilly and angry all at the same time. I felt we were squatters who had broken in and disturbed the atmosphere. The atmosphere had broken into me and squatted me. I tried not to notice my own fear and disturbance and said nothing. In the daytime I distracted myself by proposing walks along the beach, along the cliffs, through the woods. At night, back in the house, when darkness fell, I felt terrified. Cold dread filled me. Cold, cobwebby air pressed against the back of my neck. I hardly dared to move or speak. Doors would suddenly fly open and then bang shut, yet there was no draught. At breakfast one morning, glancing at the pot of Marmite (brought from England) I saw the yellow lid rise up into the air, move sideways, hover, then drop onto the cloth. Brigitte had always mocked English food; was she mocking it still? Was it a poltergeist? That night in bed I could not sleep. In the middle of the night we heard a tremendous crash along the corridor. Jim went to check. The heavy, ornate mirror in the spare room had fallen from its hook on the wall. Shards of glass littered the floor.

I never again stayed in Brigitte's house. The person who eventually bought it apparently said to my mother 'Is this house haunted? It feels as though it is.' My rational, intellectual mother briskly dismissed such nonsense.

Afterwards, I found an explanation. My grief contained a lot of anger, which I couldn't admit to at the time because I was so ashamed of it. Anger at my beloved aunt for dying, anger remembered from strictly-disciplined childhood in this house, and, most shameful, anger at not being able to inherit my aunt's property. The angry ghost was myself. I had to name her, take her back inside me, give her a safe home in my imagination.

Rosemary Badcoe
Calando *

Strange, that after playing for so long
her fingers stiffen, will not reach the chord.
He taps the beat impatiently; she stutters
past semiquavers, minims, excuses,
manages an *arpeggio*. Later,
alone, *larghetto,* she notes how
passages she learned with ease
snag on shreds of air. Downstairs
her son ascends the scales, is already
in altissimo. She hears them laugh,
imagines they rise above the orchestra,
past concert pitch, escape her range
of hearing. As she puts away the score,
her fingers pause in the high, thin air.

falling away

David Devanny
Fine Paper is Sold in the Bazaar

Translated from Mian Muhammad Bakhsh's *Saif-ul-Muluk*

Allah – my peace and refuge –
your light is inextinguishable.

Troubles are in the mind of men
in prayer no troubles remain –

to talk of eternity
in this fleeting world

is to cook fine sweets
for the jackals.

> For now the nightingale sings in the garden
> > it is passing.
> For now is the enjoyment of spring and spring
> > it is passing.
> For now is Mother, Father, beauty, youth, the company of friends,
> > all of it is passing.
> For now the waterfowl paddles; for now the water is high
> > and it is passing.
> For now pretty girls braid their hair and go out in lipstick
> > it is passing.
> For now we carry our brothers to the grave
> (soon we follow our brothers to the grave) – time –
> > it is passing.
> For now we paint our palms red with henna.
> For now our bangles sound as we sit side by side
> > it is passing.
> For now fine paper is sold in the bazaar – the city is bustling
> – even the flow of the river
> > it is passing.

O how many times
have I broken my oath to you, Allah?

Let me turn my back on vice again
and Forgiver – forgive me!

How can I be forgiven
with dark sin in my face – as it is?

How can I, but a convict,
be raised up?

> For now the branches are green
> > it is passing.
> For now there are flowers outside
> > it is passing.

Oh Allah! Let me turn away from all this –
let me know only One, see only One, say and see only One!

You are the gardener of spring's immortal flowers,
whose fragrance I have yet to smell.

Without mortal doom at the appointed hour
the soul would be trapped in this transient world,

but with it – so our longings are fulfilled:
immeasurable, ineffable and infinite.

Margaret Lewis
Tattie Keel

In the grass and the wind
and the bare earth,
in the smell of the rowans
and the wet heather,
through the soak of the rain
and the sound of the sheep
the shape of the bones remains.

Notes on Contributors

Joanne Ailward-Irwin

After taking a break from teaching to raise a family, Jo decided it was time to turn all the notes, travelogues, scraps and ideas she'd been storing into completed creative pieces. She is in the process of completing a novel for teenagers but also writes poetry, short stories and scripts.

Rosemary Badcoe

Rosemary Badcoe walks the moors and argues about the nature of consciousness. She has been published in various magazines and anthologies, most recently *Fourteen Magazine* and *Other Poetry*. She is editor of the online poetry magazine *Antiphon* http://antiphon.org.uk and moderator of the poetry forum *Poets' Graves*.

David Buckley

David Buckley, a former Head of English, has had plays on Radio 4, reviewed fiction for *The Observer* and written for *The Independent, New Statesman* and *Guardian*. Living in Sheffield, he began the MA in 2009 and is working on *Stone and Water*, a crime novel set in 1950s Bradford.

Sarah Butler

Sarah Butler writes novels and short fiction and has a particular interest in the relationship between writing and place. Her debut novel, *Ten Things I've Learnt About Love*, will be published by Picador in February 2013 and in twelve other countries around the world. You can find out more at www.sarahbutler.org.uk and www.urbanwords.org.uk.

Matt Clegg

Matt Clegg's publications include *Nobody Sonnets* (2006), *Officer* (2007), *Edgelands* (2008) and *Lost Between Stations* (2011), all from Longbarrow Press. He teaches creative practice at Derby University and poetry and autobiographical writing at Sheffield University's Institute of Lifelong Learning.

David Devanny

David Devanny was born in Bradford in 1988 where he is a member of the Beehive Poetry Group. He co-runs *The New Fire Tree Press*, a specialist poetry publisher based in Yorkshire. His own work has been published in a variety of magazines and anthologies including *Poetry Review* and *The London Magazine*.

Ian Duhig

Ian Duhig has written six books of poetry, most recently *Pandorama* (Picador 2010). He has won a Forward Prize, the National Poetry Competition twice and three times been shortlisted for the T.S. Eliot Prize.

Suzannah Evans

Suzannah Evans lives in Leeds and her pamphlet *Confusion Species* was a winner in the 2011 Poetry Business book and pamphlet competition. From 2009-2012 she was poetry editor of *Cadaverine*, an online magazine for writers under the age of 30.

Kirsty Fisher

Kirsty Fisher is from Barnsley. After a short spell of travel writing she decided to do the MA in Writing at SHU, majoring in writing for children. *Franko and the Fishheads* is now available on Kindle, and the third and final book in the trilogy, *The Four Toes of the Crillean Quest,* is almost complete.

Linda Fulton

After studying English at Chester College, Linda Fulton embarked on a teaching career in Leeds where until recently she was Assistant Head of a primary school. While her focus on the MA course is the short story, she is currently redrafting a first novel set in her native South Yorkshire.

Lesley Glaister

Lesley Glaister is the author of twelve novels, most recently *Chosen*. Her stories have been anthologised and broadcast on Radio 4. She has written drama for radio and stage. Lesley is a Fellow of the RSL, teaches creative writing at the University of St Andrews and resides in Edinburgh.

Joshua Holt

Joshua Holt is a photographer who explores connections between the medium of photography and his passion for historical research. His recent projects have delved into marginalised aspects of his hometown of Sheffield. This work has been published and exhibited and won *Granta Magazine's* 'Britain' competition.

Karl Hurst

Karl Hurst lives and works in Sheffield.

Mark Kirkby

Mark Kirkby's work has been performed on stages across the region, and includes *Bus* and *Endstories* (both at West Yorkshire Playhouse). He is co-founder of the Leeds-based new writing company *Landfill*, and has worked as a script reader for Nottingham Playhouse.

Andy Koller

Andy Koller has been writing scripts for the past ten years and has had a number of them performed in venues around South Yorkshire and beyond. His writing is concerned with characters with a slightly skewed logic, and as such his writing has been variously described as 'surreal', 'interesting' and 'well formatted'.

Margaret Lewis

Margaret Lewis lives in Sheffield but loves the hills and edits a magazine for long distance cyclists.

Carola Luther

Carola Luther is currently Poet in Residence at the Wordsworth Trust. She was born in South Africa and lives in Calderdale. Her first collection, *Walking the Animals* (Carcanet), was shortlisted for the Forward Prize for First Collection in 2004. Her second collection, *Arguing with Malarchy* (Carcanet), was published in 2011.

Suzanne McArdle

Suzanne McArdle lives in Leeds where she writes poetry and prose. Her work appeared in *Matter 11* and the recent *Grist* anthology *A Complicated Way of Being Ignored*. She is currently completing her second novel, a psychological thriller called *Bone Lake*, which will appear in *The Best of MA Writing 2012*.

Fay Musselwhite

Fay Musselwhite is working toward her final submission for the MA Writing. She collaborates locally with artists in film, sound and other media. Her poetry, which maps humans' negotiation with the elements, is published in magazines and frequently performed.

Mary Musselwhite

Mary Musselwhite came to Sheffield from the south coast three years ago, studied photography at Norton College, and is now studying for an art degree at Hallam University. She works mainly in textiles and photography, and has had artwork displayed in gallery spaces around the city.

Ruth Palmer

Ruth Palmer has written numerous short films and is currently working on a feature length screenplay. Her scripts tell stories of gritty social realism, but always with a hint of mystery and/or magic.

Matthew Rhodes

Matthew Rhodes was born in Chesterfield and went on to study English Literature, Creative Writing and Practice at Lancaster University. He has now lived in Sheffield for just under a year and is currently studying MA Writing at Sheffield Hallam University. He mainly writes short fiction with a surreal twist.

Michèle Roberts

Michèle Roberts has published novels, short stories, essays, artists' books and poetry. She is half-French and half-English. She is currently Visiting Professor at Sheffield Hallam.

Kate Rutter

Kate Rutter is co-editor of *Matter 12*. Her recent credits as an actor include *The Arbor, Oranges and Sunshine* and the forthcoming *Railway Man*, starring Nicole Kidman and Colin Firth. Her poems have been published in *Magma, Matter 10* and *11* and *Best of MA Writing 2012*. She was shortlisted for the 2010 Bridport Prize.

Mark Thorpe

Mark Thorpe started writing in his early twenties and had interest in his first novel from Faber & Faber. Following a short period writing sitcoms, he took a ten year break from writing to work in a normal job and bring up children. *Cold Breath of Summer* is due for completion in January 2013.

Jenny Vernon

Jenny Vernon spent her 20s between Ottawa, Montreal, Canada's Atlantic Provinces, and Igloolik and Baffin Island, Nunavut. She managed Gainsborough Old Hall and Lincoln Castle for Lincolnshire Museums. Jenny received her Master's at Hallam this year and is currently collaborating with anthropologist Nancy Wacowich updating and sharing her arctic fieldwork. *Stone House II* is on its way.

Photographs